HOLY WARRIORS
The Abolitionists
and American Slavery

Also by James Brewer Stewart

Joshua R. Giddings and the Tactics of Radical Politics

HOLY

The Abolitionists

Consulting Editor: Eric Foner

WARRIORS

and *American* Slavery

JAMES BREWER STEWART

AMERICAN CENTURY SERIES

HILL and WANG   New York

A division of Farrar, Straus and Giroux

Copyright © 1976 by James Brewer Stewart
All rights reserved
Published simultaneously in Canada
by McGraw-Hill Ryerson Ltd., Toronto
ISBN (clothbound edition): 0–8090–5519–8
ISBN (paperback edition): 0–8090–0123–3
Printed in the United States of America
Designed by Paula Wiener
Tenth printing, 1989
Library of Congress Cataloging in Publication Data

Stewart, James Brewer.
  Holy warriors.
(American century series)
Bibliography: p.
Includes index.
  1. Slavery in the United States—
Anti-slavery movements.   I.   Title.
E446.S83 1976   322.4′4′0973   76–22209

To my mother and father

Acknowledgments

Whatever this book's merits or defects, writing it was great fun. Those who helped make it so include: Eric Foner, who is as patient an editor as he is efficient and demanding; Dottie Stewart, who hates murky prose; my colleagues, who (by and large) left me alone to write; Mahmoud El-Kati and Norman Rosenberg, two members of the Macalester College history department who improved the manuscript with their critical attention; Ronald Walters of the Johns Hopkins University and a dozen Macalester undergraduates who did likewise. I am also beholden to the Macalester College Faculty Activities Committee and the Administrative Officers of the Newberry Library for their material assistance. To Bertram Wyatt-Brown is extended special thanks for a decade of intellectual stimulation and valued friendship.

Contents

HOLY WARRIORS
The Abolitionists
and American Slavery

Prologue:
Slavery in Republican America

In January 1863 as war between North and South raged, Wendell Phillips addressed a huge gallery of listeners in Brooklyn, New York. The audience pressed forward as this grandiloquent radical orator, "abolitionism's golden trumpet," spoke of the war's true significance and underlying cause. "It is to be a long fight," Phillips advised, "only one part of a great fight going on the world over, and which began ages ago, . . . between free institutions and caste institutions, Freedom and Democracy against institutions of privilege and class." The crowd roared its approval.

There was considerable truth in Phillips's remark. One hundred years before, hereditary systems of inequality could have been found in most parts of Western Europe and throughout the New World. Then, few had questioned the rights of seigneurial families in Europe and England to the labor of villains and serfs. Rarely had people expressed distress that France, England, Spain, Portugal, and Holland presided over rich American empires grounded upon the enslavement of black Africans. For centuries, Western Europeans had accepted the axiom that a properly ordered society respected local privileges, deprecated economic individualism, and had no place for cosmopolitan ideas about men being created equal. But in the century before Wendell Phillips spoke in Brooklyn, all these things had changed dramatically.

By 1811, the year of Phillips's birth, slavery had been all but abolished in the Northern United States. In his lifetime, he had witnessed emancipation in practically every part of Latin America. He had also observed the complex process by which states in Western Europe discarded traditional inequality for newer democratic forms. Even in Imperial Russia, the Tsar had declared gradual emancipation of the serfs. And just twenty days before this gathering in Brooklyn, President Abraham Lincoln had issued the Emancipation Proclamation, declaring that slaves in the rebel states were to be considered freed.

Whatever the forces impelling this enormous transformation in two hemispheres, the abolition of slavery in the United States was clearly central to the process. British North Americans, after all, had been the first to insist that all men are created equal. Yet by the 1840's the Southern United States had become the most formidable slave economy in the Western world. As a consequence, the federal government had increasingly evolved into a defender of slaveholders' interests in domestic politics and international affairs. But by 1863 Phillips was predicting to his audience that "the South is to be annihilated," that the slaveholding "aristocracy of the skin which considers the Declaration of Independence a sham and democracy a snare" was about to be obliterated. As Phillips was fully aware, one of the last examples of an older order, established in the days of Europe's seventeenth-century empires, was finally being eclipsed by a more modern and dynamic society.

Before the American Revolution, Wendell Phillips's father never would have predicted this outcome. Almost everywhere, slavery had proven a preeminently workable, highly profitable way of organizing agriculture. On British- and French-held Caribbean islands such as Jamaica, Bermuda, Trinidad, and Santo Domingo, cohesive slaveowning classes and immense numbers of blacks produced staggering amounts of sugar, tobacco, and rum. Spain's and Portugal's slave systems in Latin America furnished many of the same commodities, as well as a treasure of precious metals. The African slave trade, stimulated by these booming profits, had itself expanded into an intensely competitive enterprise. By the 1770's, Africans by the hundreds of thousands were used to transform many parts of the New World into plantation societies. The thirteen British colonies on the North American mainland were no exception. Even as they were declaring their independence, every colony, north and south, maintained some form of black slavery.

In colonial New England the use of slaves was common, but subject to extreme regional variation. Rural New Englanders seldom developed any contact with the system, which was largely restricted to the coastal cities. In Rhode Island, New York, New Jersey, Pennsylvania, and Delaware, by contrast, slavery had taken firm root in the countryside by the opening of the eighteenth century; in each of these colonies significant profits rewarded the master who employed slaves resourcefully on large farms. As the economy of the region grew more sophisticated, slaves adapted their labor to manufacturing enterprises. Yet slaveholding was never essential to the colonial North's economy of freehold farming, trade, and local manufacturing. During the eighteenth century, the number of Northern blacks, free or enslaved, was less than sixty thousand—a small fraction of the white population. These conditions help to explain why emancipation in the North could be accomplished with a minimum of ideological conflict.

In most of the Southern colonies, far different circumstances obtained. From the Maryland and Virginia tidewater to the Georgia frontier, slavery had always influenced nearly every aspect of the region's economic life, social customs, and political institutions. English colonists throughout North America proved willing exploiters of slave labor. But those who established slavery in the Southern colonies slowly created a distinctive culture which contrasted sharply with that of the North.

The initial development of Southern slavery was far more accidental than premeditated. The earliest white settlers had harbored no aspirations of becoming masters, but they had carried with them deep prejudices against people with black skin. These biases, which sprang from a combination of religious preoccupation, aesthetic preferences, and cultural predilections, were reinforced by the harshness of pioneer life on the Southern frontier. Black people, first imported to Virginia and Maryland as unwilling laborers but not as legally defined slaves, quickly came to serve as objects of negative self-definition for white settlers who were trying to make sense of their new circumstances. For example, the Africans' blackness, symbolizing sin, affirmed by visual contrast the white colonists' sanctified state. Soon a cycle of debasement and exploitation had taken hold; by the 1660's, black laborers in Virginia and Maryland found themselves transformed by law into hereditary slaves. Meanwhile, Spanish and Portuguese colonists in the Caribbean were demonstrating just how lucrative plantation slavery could be, and the institution then spread rapidly throughout the mainland South. The entrepreneurs who founded the Carolina colonies in the later seventeenth century thus made provision for slaveholding. In Georgia the colony's sponsors first tried to exclude slavery, but failed as settlers flouted these restrictions in favor of planting tobacco and rice. As the eighteenth century opened, slave labor seemed to most whites in the South prerequisite for order, liberty, and prosperity, for it guaranteed that the planters would never be faced with a rebellious population of lower-class whites. White freedom, in this important sense, had come to depend on black slavery. Indeed, John R. Alden has estimated that at the time of the American Revolution a full thirty-five out of every hundred Southern inhabitants were of African ancestry; blacks accounted for thirty to forty percent of those living in Maryland, Virginia, and North Carolina. In some coastal areas of colonial South Carolina, blacks outnumbered whites by as much as five to one, as natural increases among settled slaves and continuous infusions from Africa were easily absorbed by the burgeoning cash-crop system.

These large numbers of slaves led to complex and important economic and social relationships among whites. Every Southern colony prior to the Revolution contained elite groups of large slaveholders, often related by marriage, who dominated the political process, controlled the economy, and defined social norms. In Virginia and Maryland, none could doubt the success of the Lees, Dulaneys, Byrds, Carters, Custises, and other opulent "first families" in fashioning political supremacy from their scores of slaves and thousands of acres. In the Carolinas and Georgia, ambitious planter families, especially the rice and sugar "nabobs" of the coastal areas, also succeeded in their quest for dominance. Aristocratic in bearing, taste, and outlook, these eighteenth-century planters set the pattern for the next generations of slaveholders, who were to speak against radical abolitionists like Wendell Phillips during the conflicts which led to civil war. Clearly these rural magnates retained dominion by exercising the prerogative of family lineage and inherited status. In their society, egalitarian concepts such as "individualism," "democracy," and "equality" were subordinate to the dictates of local custom. The world of the planter depended on a clear ordering of unequals, and was supported by traditions of mastery and obedience.

To some extent, whites in every other stratum of Southern society also came to feel the influence of the planter elites. From the Revolution until the Civil War, small slaveowners, nonslaveowning farmers, and other poor whites always constituted a majority of the South's Caucasian population. But within this broad sector there was great variation. Prosperous farmers, often of Quaker, Moravian, or Scotch-Irish descent, usually chose to remain in the upper South, well removed from the large plantations. In Delaware, eastern Maryland, northern and eastern Virginia, and elsewhere, family farming and commercial activity, not slave-based planting, constituted the primary economic activity. Removed from the planters' dominance, these freeholders and artisans prized the virtues of self-reliance as they established small towns and farmsteads on the peripheries of the plantation economy. During the Revolution and afterward, antislavery feeling would be common in these areas.

In the Deep South, however, where the large slaveholders held preeminence, life was usually quite different for the lesser white majority. Here the planters often controlled desirable farmlands close to their residences, and ambitious freeholders found it difficult to rise in society. Instead, many small landowners emulated their "betters" by cultivating small plots of tobacco and vegetables with the help of one or two slaves. Some of these enterprises supported prosperous ways of life. Other small slaveholders spent lifetimes scratching out barely viable existences.

In either case, the marginal slaveholders and poor whites added significant dimensions to the customs of inequality in plantation society. For the most part, these lesser whites felt deep affinities with the elite planters, while regarding their economic dominance with jealous awe. Class tensions and family hostilities were always present, but other forces counterbalanced them. Complex family ties between and among large planters, small slaveholders, and other poor whites fostered communal instincts and shared social beliefs. The planter's sense of noblesse oblige toward his "inferiors," black and white alike, was built on such ties and bound the classes together.

Undergirding all these attributes of the plantation South was the primary relationship between masters and slaves, as individuals and as groups. Long before 1776 the identities of all people in the Deep South, black and white, rich and poor, had been shaped by the experiences of ownership and bondage, privilege and exploitation, patriarchy and dependence. Given this pervasive interaction, all proposals for emancipation were met with implacable hostility from every stratum of the white population. By 1776 the Virginia tobacco elites, the Carolina lowland squires, and many lesser whites had come to share a profoundly ironic fate. Long before republican American colonists began to demand independence from England and proclaim all men equal in their "inalienable rights," slavery had become the central feature of the Southerners' way of life.

In the midst of the Civil War, Wendell Phillips no longer found it useful to jeer at these glaring inconsistencies. For years he had protested his fellow citizens' eagerness simultaneously to applaud democracy and condone slavery. By this late hour, however, abolitionists had made these points far too often to bear repeating. Besides, the Emancipation Proclamation seemed to guarantee a final end to slavery. Back in 1776, however, the paradoxes and inconsistencies inherent in upholding slavery while proclaiming liberty in America had seemed both new and disturbing. By the late colonial period, the dramatic and often violent process of dismantling old slave empires in a dynamic new world had been set in motion. Nearly ninety years later, as Phillips contemplated some of the results—the Civil War and the Emancipation Proclamation—he remarked to his Brooklyn audience that "our Revolution began in 1775 and never [since] was the country left in peace." Regarding the problem of slavery, there was considerable justification for his statement.

1

Abolitionism in
Early America

"How is it that we hear the loudest *yelps* for liberty from the drivers of negroes?" taunted Samuel Johnson, one of England's most pungent opponents of American independence. His was an especially telling observation, considering that the man who declared "Give me liberty or give me death," Patrick Henry, was one of Virginia's principal slaveowners. For hundreds of years, Westerners had felt little discomfort over treating people as possessions. But on the eve of the American Revolution, as Johnson's jibe suggests, many in England and America had begun to feel uneasy about slavery. Within the British Empire, and especially in the Northern colonies, antislavery feelings suddenly seemed to run deep, and in many new directions, undercutting traditional rationalizations.

To be sure, earlier generations of colonists had never been wholly without antislavery spokesmen. Before the eighteenth century, small Quaker communities had agonized over the conflict between holding slaves and trying to live "by the light of Divine Truth." Puritan Judge Samuel Sewall in 1700 had also felt "called of God" to compose an antislavery statement, *The Selling of Joseph.* But such expressions had evoked no broad response. Seventy years later, many Quakers had freed their slaves, and politicians spoke often against the horrors of the African slave trade. Many active abolition societies petitioned governments to enact emancipation bills and to ease restrictions against individual manumissions. Slaves, too, were purchasing and suing for freedom on their own. By the 1790's, legislation for the gradual extinction of slavery was being enacted or considered in every Northern state. The idea of owning slaves had obviously become extremely repugnant to many white Americans.

Several factors were responsible for this transformation. One of them was the influence of the European Enlightenment. As colonial society matured, many Europeans were beginning to substitute the tenets of rationalism for older Christian conceptions about man and the universe. Instead of seeing man's behavior as dominated by original sin, and the cosmos as manipulated by a capricious God, philosophers stressed the supremacy of fixed natural laws which man could discover by using his intellect. Human reason, not divine revelation, became the key to knowledge; man could rationally understand the workings of nature and thereby improve himself and his society. Notions like these certainly seemed sensible to a colonial people who saw themselves transforming a wilderness into a rich, progressive civilization. One effect of such thinking was to erode traditional justifications for slavery.

Most important, Christian sanctions for enslavement, such as belief in God's unknowable will and in original sin, began to appear suspect to Americans who now felt that institutions ought to be purged of "superstition." Moreover, slavery could be judged by standards of rationalism as a relic of barbarous feudalism. To be sure, Enlightenment ideas by no means led automatically to abolitionist conclusions. John Locke, for example, experienced little difficulty in defending slavery while expounding on man's "natural rights" to freedom. Moreover, Enlightenment thinkers stressed step-by-step social change, a strong defense of private property, and sometimes the view that present customs always could be justified as improvements on the past. Despite such limitations, secular rationalism often did suggest a substantially altered attitude toward slavery. Without religious sanction, the submission of the slave to his master could be defended only on grounds of expedience. The Enlightenment's emphasis on each person's responsibility to reason and seek truth also could contain antislavery implications.

Yet in this "age of reason," Protestant religiosity was still as influential as secular thinking in leading eighteenth-century colonists in an antislavery direction. During the 1730's and 1740's, Americans grew accustomed to calling the religious upheavals around them the "Great Awakening." Deeply troubled by complicated economic, social, and religious tensions, many colonists gave vent to their anxieties through new expressions of emotional pietism. The result was an explosion of evangelical feeling, the first of a series of religious revivals which were to extend well into the nineteenth century. The preachers of the Great Awakening stressed several aspects of traditional Christianity; notably, man's sinful nature and God's wrathful judgment. Yet they did so while attempting to lead their listeners toward the experience of "conversion," a sudden communion with God during which a person was spiritually cleansed and reborn into a life of Christian dedication. In England and in every American colony, thousands of anxious souls

embraced "conversion," inspired by the sermons of powerful preachers like George Whitefield, Jonathan Edwards,
and William Tennent.

The crucial point was that people did see themselves as
doing their own choosing, now believing that sin and
salvation were not arbitrarily predetermined by an unknowable God. Instead, men were free to trust their feelings, to
accept salvation, and to oblige themselves to live according
to the dictates of Christian morality. It was a formula which
denied man's enslavement to sin, dramatized the value of
impulsive personal commitment, and demanded that people
take responsibility for their day-to-day actions. At the same
time, revivalism implied spiritual inclusiveness, placing
slaves closer to others in the human community. A God who
granted all mankind the choice of salvation could set little
store by race or status. Most often, these revivalists sought
to bring the slaves the spiritual freedom of God's Word, not
physical liberation from their masters. The deepest significance of evangelicalism for abolitionism lay elsewhere, in
the feelings of the converts themselves. Placing the voice of
conscience over law, free will over original sin, and human
benevolence over divine retribution, vital elements of
American Protestantism began groping toward a new vision
of spiritual and personal liberty.

First to act upon the antislavery imperatives awakened by
intuitive religion, however, were the Quakers. From the
first, Quakers stressed the absolute universality of God's
love, the brotherhood of man, and the sinfulness of physical
coercion. Such beliefs led some Quakers, including the
religion's founder, George Fox, to conclude that holding
slaves violated God's fundamental precepts. So convinced,
radical Quakers began in the seventeenth century to
remonstrate with their slaveowning fellows, arguing that to
obey the "inner light" meant taking responsibility for the

oppressed black. "Christ, I say, shed his blood for them as well as for you; and hath enlightened them as well as he hath enlightened you," Fox had warned Quaker slaveholders in 1676.

Several Quaker congregations and individuals did take abolitionist stands. In 1688, for instance, the Germantown Meeting of Pennsylvania Quakers decided that slaveowning was a moral abomination identical to theft and was a crime further compounded by adultery, since slavedealing separated wives and husbands. Demanding their slaveowning brethren to repent, emancipate, and endorse abolition, the Quakers also shuddered at the implications of slave insurrections for their pacifist creed: "Have these Negroes not as much right to fight for their freedom as you have to keep them slaves?"

But Quarterly and Yearly Meetings of Pennsylvania Quakers sidestepped the Germantowners' demands. So did Quaker gatherings in New York, New Jersey, and Rhode Island when petitions were presented from the dissident followers of the Quaker heretic George Keith, who insisted that since slavery violated the Golden Rule, people committed the sin of slaveowning if they refused to promote emancipation actively. Such feelings of deep religious guilt were quite uncommon in early Quakerism. Until the mid-eighteenth century, abolition remained a decidedly minority position among the Friends. Many continued to hold slaves. Most Quakers in Pennsylvania also tolerated, or were deeply involved in, the West Indian slave trade.

Still, like Keith and his followers, other Friends found themselves impelled to strive for abolition. Benjamin Lay and John Woolman, also religiously inspired, excoriated slaveowners and all complacent Christians as hopeless sinners. Lay, a hunchback, had been born in England and had traveled widely before settling in Pennsylvania in 1731.

Experiences in Barbados, where he and his wife had operated a store, had left Lay with a deep burden of guilt, tortured by a vivid memory of himself flogging helpless slaves whom he had accused of stealing. For the rest of his life, Lay sought atonement by practicing asceticism and decrying the apathy of fellow Quakers to slavery. Lay gave his most dramatic witness in 1738 before a Quaker meeting. As he spoke, he surprised his hostile audience by suddenly pulling from a hollowed-out book a bag full of "slave's blood," made of pokeberry squeezings. This red liquid he then squirted upon his unbelieving listeners, hoping vainly to make them feel the terrible burden of guilt for the sin of slavery. With less flamboyance and greater success, John Woolman traveled throughout the Southern colonies in the 1740's and 1750's, persuading Quakers to manumit their slaves. But such antislavery Quakers did not organize themselves into a significant movement until the 1760's when, as the American Revolution approached, they suddenly became far more numerous and found powerful support from several new quarters.

During the mid-1750's, pacifist Quakers who controlled the Pennsylvania Assembly refused to support colonial wars against the French and their Indian allies. By 1756, however, pressure for military action from frontier settlers and English authorities had become so intense that the Pennsylvania Friends withdrew from colonial government. Their decision meant abandoning William Penn's "holy experiment" of a Quaker-directed Commonwealth and led them to an agonizing search for the source of their tribulations. Warfare, persecution, and political self-exile constituted God's punishment for their many transgressions, many Quakers decided. Sensitive to the currents of the Great Awakening, they concluded that reformation required a revival of religious feeling, and they called on one another to rededicate themselves to the unadorned dictates of the "inner light." As a result, Quarterly Meetings grew increasingly receptive to John Woolman, Anthony Benezet, and others whose preachings traced the Friends' trials to their involvement with slavery.

On both sides of the Atlantic, Quaker antislavery was inextricably connected with entrepreneurial families whose fortunes were made from shipping, banking, mining, and insurance. As David B. Davis stresses, no eighteenth-century group more fully personified the rising tempo of transatlantic commercialism. In America, for example, the Pembertons (Israel, James, and John) built fortunes in the Caribbean import-export market, and Moses Brown of Philadelphia served as a director of the first Bank of the United States. Whether in London, Birmingham, New York, or Philadelphia, Quakers had come both to embody and stimulate the forces of commercial capitalism. In all spheres of activity, they strove for social efficiency, economic progress, moral benevolence, and civic-mindedness. No cluster of values could have been more antithetical to slavery. To Quakers, abolitionism was only a part, albeit a crucial part, of God's broader plan for human progress. Incorporating banks, floating stock, founding hospitals, or manumitting slaves—all helped to build a morally ordered, progressive society. Benighted slaves were to be transformed into upright workers. Indolent masters were to learn sobriety, thrift, and responsibility. Thus, while British Quakers busied themselves opposing England's slave-based interests in the West Indies, American Friends worked toward emancipation in the mainland colonies.

The importance of this international setting is hard to overemphasize in explaining the ultimate success of antislavery among American Quakers. The web of family connections, business contacts, and personal acquaintances which crossed and recrossed the North Atlantic continuously infused American Quakers with English antislavery support. English Quakers, for example, had toured the South in advance of Woolman, preaching antislavery. Even the Pennsylvania Friends' decision to withdraw from politics had been influenced by brethren visiting from England. Most of all, this transatlantic communications network furnished antislavery Friends in America with assurances of English support—in David B. Davis's words, "a confident sense of being members of an extended family." In contrast to the early days of Lay and Keith, antislavery activity in London or Philadelphia took on by the late 1750's personal significance for Quaker communities from the West Indies to New York.

Ultimately, international Quakerism exerted its powerful influence over the crucial 1758 Yearly Meeting. Here, over the opposition of slaveowning Friends, Benezet and Woolman argued successfully for a condemnation not only of the foreign and domestic slave trade but also of slavery itself. As English Quakers added a stinging indictment, the Philadelphia Meeting voted to exclude from positions of authority any who bought or sold slaves. Henceforth, proslavery Quakers were unable to dominate the politics of the Society or control its finances. Official committees were deputed at once to impress slaveholding Quakers with the imperative of emancipation. On the eve of the Constitutional Convention in 1787, it was practically impossible to locate a Quaker living north of Virginia who dealt in slaves. The Friends' efforts at self-reform had achieved impressive results. But success induced no feelings of complacency; it dictated instead that Quakers carry the battle out of the meeting house and into the larger society.

During the 1760's and 1770's, Quakers found that many Northern colonists had suddenly become receptive to their crusade. As the conflict with England approached, Americans familiarized themselves with Enlightenment ideas and put them to revolutionary purposes. Ever more sensitive to encroachments upon their traditional privileges, patriots constantly warned that oppressive English officials were conspiring to overthrow natural law and to subject them to slavery. Quoting Locke, Montesquieu, and English libertarian writers, such Americans saw themselves struggling to preserve republican government and individual liberties against corrupt England's arbitrary exercise of power. In the context of revolutionary thought, the concept of slavery thus became freighted with profound significance. When colonists employed the term with reference to English policy, they meant the destruction of a person's property, his inherent liberties, even his inclination to preserve his own autonomy. Political slavery reminded them of Old World despotisms like Turkey, Russia, and even ultimately England itself where, they believed, rational, free men were in danger of being transformed into superstitious, enervated serfs dominated by corrupt lords. Judged in a world setting, America appeared to the patriots quite literally the last bastion of liberty.

Given these perceptions, the excruciating contrast between their own inalienable rights and the powerlessness of the slave became, for some colonists, too obvious to ignore. As early as 1764 the influential James Otis of Massachusetts pondered this contrast, and his conclusions anticipated by a decade phrases which were to be commonplace on the eve of independence. Excoriating slavery as "a most shocking violation of the law of nature," a practice which "makes every dealer a tyrant," Otis denied that "any logical inference in favor of slavery" could be drawn "from a flat nose, a long or a short face." He concluded by warning that not all threats to American liberty came from abroad.

Slaveholders, "who every day barter away other men's liberty," would soon "care little for their own," Otis asserted, and would plunge government into "ferocity, cruelty and brutal barbarity." Slaveowning not only compromised the patriots' defense of American rights but threatened to subvert their liberties altogether.

As relations with England deteriorated and war ensued, many other colonial leaders began to decry slavery, using arguments like Otis's. Patrick Henry, John Adams, Alexander Hamilton, Thomas Paine, Albert Gallatin, James Madison, Thomas Jefferson, and many other august figures declared slavery a dangerous contradiction of the Revolution's aims. Hamilton, Gallatin, and Benjamin Franklin became particularly active in manumissionist circles. To be sure, not all of these individuals were convinced as Otis had been that environmental influences, not innate qualities, accounted for the disturbing "differences" perceived in black people by so many whites. Jefferson, for one, struggled in vain to square his rationalistic commitment to environmentalism with his gnawing "suspicion" (as he once described it) that blacks were by nature brutal and intellectually shallow. Yet the major significance of these espousals, as the Quakers knew, was that abolitionism was now receiving impressive support from the most prominent circles of national politics.

Evangelical Yankees in particular found themselves receptive to the idea of emancipation as a result of the crisis with England. Among New England Calvinists, political turmoil evoked apocalyptic responses that inextricably meshed the trials of the nation with the torments of the sinner. God, they admonished, was now exacting punishment for the nation's sins by using British repression as His divine instrument. Revivalists exhorted that liberty could never be preserved until all citizens had cast out their collective enslavement to worldliness and disbelief. The concepts of slavery and freedom, now endowed with cosmic meanings, led many evangelicals to regard the enslavement of blacks as the foulest of the nation's transgressions, the principal obstacle to realizing independence. Protestant demands for emancipation began to take on an urgency hitherto unknown in Western history. The religious and secular frameworks of antislavery became wholly intertwined; the differences between politicians and evangelists blurred as both emphasized the relation between abolition and independence. Samuel Hopkins, the formidable Calvinist intellectual, best embodied this fusion of religious and political ideology. Other evangelicals spoke out, joining Quakers such as Benezet and Woolman, Methodists like Francis Asbury and Thomas Coke, freethinkers like Franklin, and deists like Thomas Paine. By 1776 each of these spokesmen had given abolitionism a prominent place in his thinking. It was indeed a formidable coalition, at least in the North, which set in motion the Revolution's thrust for emancipation.

But the realities of warfare, as well as the power of ideas, also linked abolition to the Patriot cause. It became painfully difficult for evangelical ministers to counsel submissiveness among the slaves while exhorting their white parishioners to arms. Revivalists also began to fear that without abolition God would kindle insurrection among the slaves, using them, as well as the British, as instruments of divine retribution. In 1775 such prophecies appeared well-nigh fulfilled when Lord Dunmore, Virginia's Royal Governor, promised freedom to all slaves who would desert rebellious masters and serve in the king's army. Over eight hundred slaves enlisted, giving substance to Hopkins's warning that God was "so ordering it in his Providence" to induce the slaves "to take up arms against us . . . in order to get their liberty."

Likewise, slaves in the North and upper South found that they could also use the Patriot cause to good advantage. Difficulties in obtaining white volunteers led several Northern legislatures to grant freedom to slaves who fought in the militia. In Maryland, slaves were enlisted in the army. As in every subsequent American war, many whites could not stifle their guilt as blacks gave their lives in defense of the society that so thoroughly oppressed them; sympathy for emancipation became the obvious way to make amends. Perhaps sensing these anxieties a slave named Prince conveyed to the 1777 Massachusetts Assembly a petition for emancipation on behalf of "A Great Number of Blacks detained in a State of slavery in the Bowels of a free and Christian Country." In 1779 the Connecticut General Assembly received a similar memorial from Negroes living in Fairfield County. "Every Principle from which America has acted in the course of its difficulties with Great Britain pleads stronger than a thousand arguments" for emancipation, declared one group of enslaved petitioners. Free blacks joined these petition campaigns, sued in court to obtain their freedom, and also began to organize important new social agencies. By 1780, for example, the black community of Providence, Rhode Island, had its own benevolent association, and by the 1790's, blacks in the North were administering a full range of aid societies and fraternal orders. That slaves and free blacks felt encouraged to act so aggressively is perhaps the best measure of how commonplace Northern abolitionist feeling had become.

As many white attitudes passed through this transformation, Quakers intensified their own crusade. In 1774, Benezet bombarded the Continental Congress with antislavery demands and finally obtained its consent to stop all slave importations. In 1775, Philadelphia Quakers organized the first association devoted exclusively to abolition, the Society for the Relief of Free Negroes Unlawfully Held in Bondage. Sympathetic to the Quaker zeal for "useful" improvements in the name of economic progress, powerful politicians, manufacturing magnates, and lawyers—the dynamic commercial and professional sectors of Northern society—likewise took up the abolitionist cause. Only a few of these urban entrepreneurs owned slaves, and very few of the North's significant men of wealth depended on slavery for social position or economic advancement. Slaves also were too few to pose a serious threat to white supremacy if transformed into freedmen. Social harmony and economic betterment would be enhanced, it was thought, once motives for rebellion were removed by emancipation.

Under these circumstances, the forces of abolitionism proved irresistible in the end. By 1784 every Northern state save New York and New Jersey had enacted laws providing for gradual emancipation; by 1804 these states, too, had passed such bills. Of course, racism and the economic interest of the slaveholders generated movements of stubborn obstruction. Yet, for the only time in American history, abolitionists had succeeded in peacefully merging with those who controlled the levers of power. Without such impressive institutional support, abolitionists were to find that their pleas evoked much less willing responses. In most of the Revolutionary South, abolition ultimately made no headway at all.

Southern whites were no less receptive than their Northern counterparts to natural-rights thinking and evangelical humanitarianism during the Revolutionary era. Yet such influences usually suggested, not abolition, but the need to humanize slavery. Widespread criticism by Quakers, Methodists, and other religious groups did strike a modestly responsive note in some planter circles; Jefferson, Madison, and other notables supported easing restrictions on voluntary emancipation. Jefferson, of course, condemned the African slave trade in a passage which was later deleted from the Declaration of Independence. During the 1780's and early 1790's, private manumissions increased dramatically, especially in the upper South. Here, as noted, freehold farming and commercial activity, not plantation slavery, were the most common means of livelihood. With tobacco prices deflated because of soil depletion, the loss of British patronage, and the impact of warfare, slavery's hold in parts of Maryland, Virginia, and Delaware had become even weaker. Quakers spoke with enthusiasm to such hard-pressed slaveowners about the morality and economic logic of emancipation.

Some large slaveholders also made complicated provisions for the gradual release of their bondsmen as each satisfied certain requirements reflecting "fitness" for freedom. Wholesale private emancipations thus created a new and very large free Negro class. By 1810, free Southern blacks numbered well over a hundred thousand. Henceforth, they constituted a major component in the Southern economy, and a major new irritant to the slaveholders. Meanwhile, castration and other forms of mutilation as punishment were written out of the slave codes; provisos making it a crime for masters to grossly mistreat their slaves replaced them. Thus did Southern whites reflect their discomfort over maintaining slavery while struggling for national independence.

However, slavery retained its supremacy in the South, for it proved an exceptionally successful social and economic system, even in this age of revolution. Contrary to older opinions, slavery was hardly dying in the years from 1770 to 1800. Except in the border areas, prices and profits were stable. The loss of British protection, though serious, was not disastrous. Slavery paid well in the North, but in the plantation South it had reconfirmed itself as the cornerstone of the economy. Most Southern whites, moreover, could never tolerate the prospect of the huge free black population that would be created by emancipation programs which followed Northern examples.

Finally, as Edmund Morgan has suggested, it was the slaves themselves who made it so easy for elitist planters to espouse revolutionary republicanism. The powerless blacks served in the South as a substitute for and a check upon a restive white proletariat which might have otherwise applied revolutionary rhetoric to a rebellion of its own. In this sense, the Revolution embodied for Southern whites profoundly proslavery sentiments. Outside of the freehold border areas, no manumission society existed anywhere in the South; no serious proposals for emancipation reached any Southern legislature.

In this manner, the Revolution had endowed Southern slavery with a new legitimacy. But with legitimacy also came new pangs of insecurity, a tough mood of sectional defensiveness. Slaveholders had now to accustom themselves to an emerging group of "free states" that ringed their northern borders. Moreover, antislavery-minded Yankees like Benezet continued to work with a rising generation of British reformers, seeking to end slavery in the Caribbean, the American planters' southern flank. Most of all, Southern whites were aware that the Revolution had set people to begin a hitherto unprecedented questioning of slavery. Little wonder, then, that Southern leaders took a combative stance toward the 1787 Constitutional Convention and approached its deliberations keeping their slaveholding interests paramount.

Historians have sometimes asserted that the Founding

Fathers betrayed the Revolution's commitment to emancipation by failing to incorporate abolition into the Constitution. To be sure, the Philadelphia Convention contained many representatives who had identified themselves with antislavery. As the delegates met, abolitionist feeling in the North was also reaching its apogee. During this same year, the Continental Congress enacted the Northwest Ordinance, prohibiting slavery in territories north of the Ohio and east of the Mississippi rivers. Yet it is unlikely that the Founding Fathers could have placed Southern slavery on a course of extinction, even if they had wished to.

The makeup of the Convention guaranteed a direct potent voice to those determined to resist any infringements of the right to hold slaves. Southern delegates constituted a powerful bloc in the Convention, one capable of destroying the proceedings simply by walking out. To nationalist Founding Fathers, secession was to be avoided at all costs, regardless of one's dislike of slavery. The Founders, moreover, firmly believed that the Revolution's goals were intimately linked with the sanctity of private property. Emancipation by federal government coercion was thus as repugnant to them in theory as it was impossible in practice. Finally, by 1787 white citizens had come to sense the urgency of defining their newly won national citizenship, and one thing had become certain, abolitionist sentiment notwithstanding: to be genuinely American, whether Yankee or Southerner, meant possessing a white skin. Even as blacks in the North emerged from slavery, they entered a world of segregation and economic exploitation, deprived of equality before the law. Racism had long ago established itself as a vital component of the national character. Little wonder, then, that the Founding Fathers incorporated protection for the planter classes into the Constitution rather than liberation of their slaves.

The men who wrote the Constitution erected seemingly insuperable barriers against peaceful emancipation. The Founders did betray their squeamishness by avoiding the words "slave" and "slavery" in the Constitution's language. Instead, they referred to "persons." The provision which outlawed the African slave trade after 1808 also reflected genuine antislavery feeling. But in many of its clauses the document clearly upheld the "peculiar institution." For instance, Article Four affirmed the right of masters to recover runaway slaves. But, most crucially, the Constitution granted the planter class exceptional leverage in national affairs. Article One provided that three-fifths of the slave population was to be counted for purposes of taxation and representation in the House of Representatives. In this way the Constitution guaranteed slaveholders political power which exceeded significantly their actual numbers. Their authority over their black chattel drew reaffirmation from the supreme law of the land.

In succeeding years, abolitionists and politicians came to disagree strongly over the Founding Fathers' "real" attitudes toward slavery. Two points, however, seem beyond reasonable dispute. First, the Constitution itself, while clearly sanctioning slaveowning, nevertheless contained so many sectional compromises as to appear highly ambiguous to later generations. Southern secessionists and Yankee unionists, not to mention quarreling factions of abolitionists, were to find historical justifications aplenty for irreconcilable points of view about the government's power over slavery. In short, the makers of the Constitution set no framework for future discussions of slavery. Without such a legacy, the boundaries of disagreement were destined to become limitless.

A second point, less compelling in the long run perhaps, was nonetheless of much greater moment to the abolitionists of the eighteenth century. Whatever the Founders' private feelings about slavery, their primary concern lay in bringing stability out of the experience of revolution. The framers of the Constitution saw themselves struggling to guarantee the right of private property and to replace the tumults of localism with the majesty of national power. Theirs was a tough-minded posture, one which subordinated disruptive innovations like abolition to the stern demands of national republicanism. So even as Northern legislatures continued to debate emancipation bills, the Philadelphia Convention announced a new era of national consolidation and conservatism. Nationhood achieved, the North's antislavery consensus began quietly to melt away.

American responses to the French Revolution also undercut support for abolition. It appeared that in France anticlericalism, property confiscation, and political purges had overwhelmed orderly republican reform. Then the slaves of Santo Domingo began to follow the examples of their French overlords and rose in bloody revolt. By 1793, refugee planters with their slaves were converging in large numbers in Virginia as Black Jacobins in Santo Domingo continually bested French invaders. The "excesses" of white rebellion in France now seemed to have been appropriated for the purpose of black revolution. Planters restricted slave imports from the West Indies and deported free blacks, fearing, in Winthrop Jordan's phrase, that "the cancer of revolution" was being spread by provocateurs from Santo Domingo to slaves on the mainland.

Yet these fearful expectations were not unfounded, and throughout the 1790's masters could point to a high incidence of slave resistance. Toward the end of 1800, apprehension finally became fact as Virginians were confronted with authentic rebellion: Gabriel Prosser's attempt to capture Richmond with an army of slaves and spread revolt throughout the South. White revenge and rumors of black violence followed until, after more than thirty hangings, Virginia authorities finally declared the insurrection quelled. Little wonder, given this conservative spirit of the 1790's, that few demurred when in 1791 Kentucky was quietly admitted as the first new slave state to enter the Union. Two years later Congress, as authorized by the Constitution, also enacted a fugitive slave law. There were antislavery residues to be sure. In 1807, Congress passed the legislation permitted by the Constitution prohibiting Americans from participating in the international slave trade. Five years earlier, Ohio had been admitted to the Union with a constitution prohibiting slavery, as prescribed by the Northwest Ordinance. But these events hardly augured well for abolitionism. By 1810, as Eli Whitney's cotton gin opened new opportunities for the planter class, militant abolitionism in America had expired.

As antislavery feeling receded, Americans in both sections began to transfer their concerns about slavery to the American Colonization Society. Founded in 1816, the Colonization Society proposed to resettle American free blacks in Africa and encouraged voluntary emancipations. The Society attempted in this way to surmount the charge that emancipation would saddle the nation with an intolerably large, unassimilable free black population. It also suggested to Southern whites, nervous about insurrection plots, that means were available for reducing the nonslave Negro population in their neighborhoods. The idea of solving America's race problems by transporting its unwilling black inhabitants was wildly impractical, a financial and organizational impossibility. But those were not the only drawbacks. Some sensitive planters were always to oppose the idea as a subtle assault on the master-slave relationship. Most of all, blacks spurned such colonization as a racist insult, a plan concocted by white supremacists to serve their own ends. We "prefer being colonized in the most remote corner of the land of our nativity, to being exiled to a foreign country," declared free blacks from Richmond, Virginia, in 1817. When black leaders did endorse colonization, it was only because they feared that the bigotry of white America had left their race facing a future of unrelieved misery.

Despite these obstacles, colonization always held a compelling attraction to those seeking "rational" alternatives to civil war, servile insurrection, and black equality. During the 1820's, the peak years of the American Colonization Society, eminent clerics and such nationally prominent slaveowning politicians as Henry Clay, James Monroe, and John Marshall endorsed the Society's efforts to establish in Liberia a colony for transported blacks. Clearly, these men could not be considered serious abolitionists. Yet during these years, some colonizationists did believe that they were sponsoring Christian uplift of blacks while alleviating some of slavery's most objectionable features. Accordingly, they urged masters to educate their bondsmen for new lives as Christian missionaries after being selectively manumitted and transferred to Liberia. By enlightening his slaves, the master, too, was to learn Christian benevolence, thereby lessening the brutalities of slave ownership. Many colonizationists expected that popular attachments to slavery would gradually diminish, and that, perhaps, the institution itself would someday come to an end.

Here was a vision with considerable attraction for well-educated, idealistic young men anxious in the 1820's to forward the moral improvement of America's black population. Among them were an impressive number of individuals who were soon to assume preeminence in militant abolitionism. Lewis and Arthur Tappan, William Lloyd Garrison,

Joshua Leavitt, James G. Birney, Simeon S. Jocelyn, Amos A. Phelps, and Samuel J. May represent only a partial list of the abolitionists who had at first believed that colonization promised much for the black race. For them, colonization functioned as a "surrogate for antislavery" in David B. Davis's phrase, a respectable outlet for misgivings about slavery in an era which demanded ideological moderation. In this respect, the Society served as an important transition for abolitionists-to-be. Its publications acquainted them with the evils of slavery and the oppressive lot of America's free blacks. And later on, as young abolitionists renounced their adherence to gradualism, the Society became a crucial focus of youthful rebellion against traditional solutions to the problem of slavery. The American Colonization Society thus foreshadowed radical abolitionism as well as affirmed the status quo.

Although few people in the 1820's openly objected to slavery as an institution, the issue did spark serious sectional conflict and racial discontent. From 1819 to 1821, politicians flirted with secession as Congress, over Northern protests, admitted Missouri into the Union as a slave state. Organized with a state constitution upholding slavery, Missouri applied for statehood in 1819. At once, New England politicians protested that America's republican future, which lay in its Western settlements, should not be jeopardized by any expansion of slave labor. New York's James Tallmadge offered a bill which prohibited any extension of slavery into new territories, and suddenly Northern and Southern representatives found themselves in hostile opposition to one another. Even in a period when expressions of antislavery were rare, it was apparent that the issue of slavery's future in the West awakened deeply conflicting visions of the Republic's future. Compromise finally soothed this crisis when Maine was admitted as a free state along with the slave state Missouri, while slavery was excluded from Louisiana Purchase lands north of 36° 30'. Two years later, in 1821, in Charleston, South Carolina, local whites ruthlessly suppressed what they thought to be a gigantic conspiracy led by freedman Denmark Vesey. Yet these occurrences, each an undeniably serious crisis, evoked no widespread misgivings among whites about the existence of slavery itself.

At the same time, however, a complex set of forces was at work during the 1820's which soon ignited among New Englanders an abolitionist movement of unparalleled intensity. Inspired like their Puritan ancestors by Christian egalitarianism and a profound sense of personal guilt, young men and women were soon to take up the immense task of convincing their countrymen that slavery was a sin, and that race prejudice was at war with the teachings of Jesus. In so doing, they would appeal to the precedents set by the Revolution, the Declaration of Independence, the Northwest Ordinance, and the outlawing of the African slave trade. Their opponents were to point to the "three-fifths clause" and applaud the Revolution's guarantee of private property. The eighteenth century's antislavery legacy, ambiguous in the extreme, would prove quite serviceable to all participants in the debates over slavery, which ultimately led to civil war.

2

The Commitment to
Immediate Emancipation

American society in the late 1820's presented the pious,
well-informed Yankee with tremendous challenges. For the
better part of a decade, Protestant spokesmen had warned
him against the nation's all-absorbing interest in material
wealth, geographic expansion, and party politics. Infidelity,
he was told, flourished on the Western and Southern
frontiers; vice reigned supreme in the burgeoning Eastern
cities. In politics, he was exhorted to combat atheist
demagogues called Jacksonians who insisted on popular rule
and further demanded that the clerical establishment be
divorced from government. Urban workingmen and frontier
pioneers, morally numbed by alcoholism and illiteracy, were
being duped in massive numbers by the blandishments of
these greedy politicos. America, he was assured, faced moral
bankruptcy and the total destruction of its Christian
identity. Exaggerated as such claims may seem, they had
some grounding in reality. Yankee Protestantism was indeed
facing immense new challenges from a society in the throes

of massive social change. As Protestants struggled to overcome these adversities, the abolitionists' crusade for immediate emancipation also took form.

By the end of the 1820's, America was in the midst of unparalleled economic growth. Powerful commercial networks were coming to link all sections of the country; canals, mass-circulation newspapers, and (soon) railroads reinforced this thrust toward regional interdependency. Northern business depended as never before on trade with the South. The "cotton revolution" which swept the Mississippi-Alabama-Georgia frontier in turn stimulated textile manufacturing and shipping in the Northeast. In the Northwest, yet another economic boom took shape as businessmen and farmers in Ohio, Indiana, and Illinois developed lucrative relationships with the Eastern seaboard, and the population of Northern cities grew apace. Politicians organized party machines which catered to these new interests and to the "common man's" mundane preferences.

The cosmopolitan forces of economic interdependence, urbanization, democratic politics, and mass communication all posed major challenges to provincial New England culture. The Protestant response, in John L. Thomas's apt phrase, was "to fight democratic excess with democratic remedies." Throughout the 1820's New Englanders mounted an impressive counterattack against the forces of "immorality" by commandeering the tools of their secular opponents: the printing press, the rally, and the efficiently managed bureaucratic agency. With the hope of renovating American religious life, the American Tract Society spewed forth thousands of pamphlets which exhorted readers to repent. The Temperance Union carried a similar message to the nation's innumerable hard drinkers. Various missionary societies sent witnesses to back-country settlements, the waterfront haunts of Boston's seamen, the bordellos of New York City. These societies envisioned a reassertion of traditional New England values on a national scale. At the same time, although unintentionally, these programs for Christian restoration were stimulating in pious young men and women stirrings of spiritual revolt.

All of these reform enterprises drew their vitality from revivalistic religion. Once again, social discontent and political alienation found widespread expression through the conversion experience; the Great Revivals announced the Protestant resurgence of the 1820's. Like their eighteenth-century predecessors, powerful evangelists such as Charles G. Finney and Lyman Beecher urged their audiences that man, though a sinner, should nonetheless strive for holiness and choose a new life of sanctification. Free will once again took precedence over original sin, which was again redefined as voluntary selfishness. As in the 1750's, God was pictured as insisting that the "saved" perform acts of benevolence, expand the boundaries of Christ's kingdom, and recognize a personal responsibility to improve society. Men and women again saw themselves playing dynamic roles in their own salvation and preparing society for the millennium. By the thousands they flocked to the Tract Society, the Sunday School Union, the temperance and peace organizations, and the Colonization Society. Seeking prevention, certainly not revolution, evangelicals thus dreamed of a glorious era of national reform: rid of liquor, prostitution, atheism, and popular politics, the redeemed masses of America would gladly submit to the leadership of Christian statesmen. So blessed, Americans would no longer fall prey to the blandishments of that hard-drinking gambler, duelist, and unchurched slaveowner, President Andrew Jackson.

From this defensive setting sprang New England's cru-

sade against slavery. Indeed, radical reformers of all varieties, not just abolitionists, traced their activism to the
revivals of the 1820's. As we have seen, revivalism had also
given powerful impetus to abolitionism in the eighteenth
century. History was hardly repeating itself, however. The
revivals of the Revolutionary era had not generated sustained movements for radical change. By contrast, the
evangelical outbursts of the 1820's fostered alienation and
rebellion among thousands of young men and women. The
result was a bewildering variety of projects for reform.

Several factors help to explain this difference. For one
thing, the revivalists of the 1820's found it impossible to
define specific sources for the immorality that so disturbed
them. There was no tyrannical king or corrupt Parliament to
focus upon. There was also no glorious political brotherhood
to join, such as the Sons of Liberty, no exalted goal to
achieve, such as permanent independence from England. In
short, the evangelical crusaders of the 1820's had few stable
points of reference upon which to fix. Few institutions or
popular leaders commanded their loyalties. Lacking these,
revivalists sensed that infidelity could issue from any source,
that corruption crowded in from all quarters. Their own
dedication was all that stood between a sinning nation and
God's all-consuming retribution. Here was a temperament
which urged a lifetime of intense Christian struggle and a
searching reexamination of accepted American institutions.
The potential for radical commitment was indeed enormous.

While revivalism's ambiguities stimulated anxiety in the
1820's, its network of benevolent agencies opened opportunities for young Americans which their eighteenth-century
counterparts could never have foreseen. The missionary
agencies and even the revivals themselves were organized
along complex bureaucratic lines. Volunteers were always

needed to drum up donations or to organize meetings. New careers were also created. For the first time in American history, young people could regard social activism as a legitimate profession. Earnest ministerial candidates began accepting full-time positions as circuit riders, regional agents, newspaper editors, and schoolteachers, with salaries underwritten by the various benevolent agencies. One important abolitionist-to-be, Joshua Leavitt, spent his first years after seminary editing the *Seaman's Friend*, an evangelical periodical for sailors. Another, Elizur Wright, Jr., was employed by the American Tract Society.

Most important to abolitionism was the effect of revivalism on the ministry itself. Once open to only an elite, the ministry had by the 1820's become a common profession. Spurred by expanding geography, seminaries increased their enrollments as they attracted young New Englanders who burned to aid in America's regeneration. Included were some destined to number among abolitionism's dominant figures: Samuel J. May, Amos A. Phelps, Theodore D. Weld, Joshua Leavitt, and Stephen S. Foster, to name only a few. First as seminarians, then as volunteers, paid agents, clergymen, and teachers, many pious young Americans dedicated themselves to fighting sin and disbelief. Given the intensity of the evangelical temperament, the results of such experiences were to suggest, to some, far more radical courses of action, and there can be no question that these abolitionists-to-be took their responsibilities in deadly earnest.

There is some persuasive evidence that family background and upbringing predisposed young New Englanders toward a radical outlook. Over twenty years ago, David Donald gathered information which suggests the influence of parental guidance on abolitionism's most prominent spokesmen. Abolitionism, he reported, was a revolt of youth raised by old New England families of farmers, teachers, ministers, and businessmen. The parents of abolitionists were usually well-educated Presbyterians, Congregationalists, Quakers, and Unitarians who participated heavily in revivalism and its attendant benevolent projects. Many scholars have effectively criticized Donald's methods and have raised serious questions about the reliability of his evidence regarding the movement's rank-and-file. Donald also erred in concluding that commitments to abolitionism were reactions to a loss of social status to nouveau riche neighbors. Actually, abolitionism flourished among groups with rising social prospects during the 1830's. Nevertheless, Donald's findings remain extremely suggestive as to the influence of parental guidance on abolitionism's most prominent leaders.

In such families, as numerous biographers have since attested, a stern emphasis on moral uprightness and social responsibility generally prevailed. In the words of Bertram Wyatt-Brown, young men and women "learned that integrity came not from conformity to the ways of the world, but to the principles by which the family tried to live." Parents were usually eager to inculcate a high degree of religious and social conscience. In their reminiscences, abolitionists commonly paid homage to strong-minded mothers or fathers whose intense religious fervor dominated their households. In his early years, Wendell Phillips constantly turned to his mother for instruction, and after her death he confessed that "whatever good is in me, she is responsible for." Thomas Wentworth Higginson, Arthur and Lewis Tappan, and William Lloyd Garrison became, like Phillips, leading abolitionists and also internalized the religious dictates of dominating mothers. Sidney Howard Gay, James G. Birney, Elizur Wright, Jr., and Elijah P. Lovejoy are examples of abolitionists who modeled their early lives to fit the intentions of exacting fathers. Young women who were to enter the movement usually sought the advice of their fathers, as in the cases of Elizabeth Cady Stanton and Maria Weston Chapman. Yet whatever the child's focus, the expectations of parents seldom varied. Displays of conscience and upright behavior brought the rewards of parental love and approval.

Children also learned that sexual self-control was a vital part of righteous living. Parents stressed prayer and benevolent deeds as substitutes for "carnal thoughts" and intimacy; they associated sexual sublimation with family stability and personal redemption. During his years at boarding school and later at Harvard, Wendell Phillips strove to satisfy his mother on all these counts. Lewis Tappan, too, remembered how hard he had worked "to be one of the best scholars, often a favorite with the masters, and a leader among the boys in our plays." When he was twenty and living away from home, Tappan still received admonitions from his mother about the pitfalls of sex. Recalling a dream, she wrote, "Methought you had, by frequenting the theatre, been drawn into the society of lewd women, and had contracted a disease that was preying upon your constitution." For his part, Tappan had already sworn to "enjoy a sound mind and body, untainted by vice." A strong sense of their individuality, a deadly earnestness about moral issues, confidence in their ability to master themselves and to improve the world—these were the qualities which so often marked abolitionists in their early years. Above all, these future reformers believed in their own superiority and fully expected to become leaders.

Of course, not all children of morally assertive New England parents became radical abolitionists. William Lloyd Garrison's brother, for example, emerged from his mother's tutelage and lapsed into alcoholism. Still, the

predisposition to rebellion remains hard to dismiss. Alienation and self-doubt certainly ran especially deep among
these sensitive, socially conscious young people. Besides,
America in the 1820's appeared to many a complex and
bewildering place. Certain social realities were soon to seem
disturbingly at variance with their high expectations and
fixed moral codes.

These future abolitionists entered young adulthood at a
time when rapid mobility, technological advance, and
dizzying geographic expansion were transforming traditional institutions. Those who took up pastorates, seminary
study, or positions in benevolent agencies were shocked to
discover that the Protestant establishment was hardly free
from the acquisitive taint and bureaucratic selfishness that
they had been brought up to disdain. Expecting to lead
communities of godfearing, Christian families, young ministers like Amos A. Phelps, Elizur Wright, Jr., and Charles T.
Torrey confronted instead a fragmented society of entrepreneurs. Theodore Dwight Weld, for example, wrote critically
to the great evangelist Charles G. Finney that "*revivals* are
fast becoming with you a sort of trade, to be worked at so
many hours a day." Promoters of colonization, such as
James G. Birney and Joshua Leavitt, became increasingly
disturbed that many of their co-workers were far less
interested in Christian benevolence than in ridding the
nation of inferior blacks. In politics, Lewis Tappan, William
Jay, and William Lloyd Garrison searched desperately and
without success for a truly Christian leader, an alternative
to impious Andrew Jackson and the godless party he led.

Predictably, misgiving became ever more frequent among
young evangelicals. They began to question their abilities, to
rethink their choices of career, and to doubt the Christianity
of the churches, seminaries, and benevolent societies. Just
possibly, the nation was far more deeply mired in sin than

anyone had imagined. Just possibly, parental formulas for godly reformation were fatally compromised. And, most disturbing of all, just possibly the idealist-reformer himself needed reforming—a new relationship with God, a new vision of his responsibility as a Christian American.

The powerful combination in the 1820's of Yankee conservatism, revivalist benevolence, New England upbringing, and social unrest was leading young evangelicals toward a genuinely radical vision. Given this setting, it hardly seems surprising that a militant abolitionist movement began to take shape. Opposition to slavery certainly constituted a dramatic affirmation of one's Christian identity and commitment to a life of Protestant purity. Economic exploitation, sexual license, gambling, drinking and dueling, disregard for family ties—all traits associated with slaveowning—could easily be set in bold contrast with the pure ideals of Yankee evangelicalism.

There were a few militant antislavery spokesmen in the upper South in the 1820's, but their influence on young New Englanders was negligible. The manumission societies organized largely by evangelical Quakers and Moravian Brethren in Tennessee, Kentucky, and other border areas were already collapsing at the start of New England's crusade for immediate emancipation. The Southern antislavery movement's chief spokesman, editor Benjamin Lundy, had retreated northward from Tennessee. By 1829 he was living in Baltimore and had hired a zealous young editorial assistant from Newburyport, Massachusetts: William Lloyd Garrison.

The sudden emergence of immediate abolitionism in New England thus cannot be explained as a predictable offshoot of Yankee revivalism or a legacy from the upper South. Instead, one must emphasize the interaction between the rebellious feelings of these religious men and women and the events of the early 1830's. As the 1830's opened in an atmosphere of crisis, their attentions became intensely fixed on slavery. As in the early 1820's, the nation was again beset by black rebellions and threats of southern secession. Concurrently, events in England and in its sugar islands empire seemed to confirm the necessity of demanding the immediate emancipation of all slaves, everywhere. An unprecedented array of circumstances and jarring events suddenly converged on these anxious young people and launched them upon the lifetime task of abolishing slavery.

By far the most alarming was the ominous note of black militancy on which the new decade opened. In Boston in 1829, an ex-slave from North Carolina, David Walker, published the first edition of his famous *Appeal*. A landmark in black protest literature, Walker's *Appeal* condemned colonization as a white supremacist hoax, excoriated members of his own race for their passivity, and called, as a last resort, for armed resistance. "I do declare," wrote Walker, "that one good black man can put to death six white men." Whites had never hesitated to kill blacks, he advised, so "if you commence . . . do not trifle, for they will not trifle with you." Other events, even more shocking, were to follow. In 1831, William Lloyd Garrison, now living in Boston, issued a call for immediate emancipation in the *Liberator*. Soon after, Southampton County, Virginia, erupted in the bloody Nat Turner insurrection, the largest slave revolt in antebellum America. Still another massive slave rebellion broke out in British Jamaica in 1831. Coinciding with these racial traumas was the Nullification Crisis of 1831–32, a confrontation ignited by South Carolina's opposition to national tariff policy and by the deeper fear that the federal government might someday abolish slavery. Intent on preserving state sovereignty and hence slavery, South Carolina politicians led by John C. Calhoun temporarily defied national authority, threatened secession, and risked occupation by federal troops.

As these frightening events unfolded, young evangelicals cast aside their self-doubt. Unfocused discontent gave way to soul-wrenching commitments to eradicating the sin of slavery. The combined actions of Nat Turner, the South Carolina "Nullifiers," and David Walker suggested with dramatic force that slavery was the fundamental cause of society's degraded state. As Theodore D. Weld observed, the abolitionist cause "not only *overshadows* all others, but . . . absorbs them into itself. Revivals, moral Reform etc. will remain stationary until the temple is cleansed." The step-by-step solutions advocated by their parents suddenly appeared to invite only God's retribution. Like Garrison, Arthur Tappan, and many others, James G. Birney sealed his commitment to immediate abolition by decrying colonization. The Colonization Society, Birney charged, acted as "an opiate to the consciences" of those who would otherwise "feel deeply and keenly the sin of slavery."

In one sense, these sudden espousals of immediate abolition can be understood as a strategic innovation developed because of the manifest failures of gradualism. Slaveholders had certainly shown no sympathy to moderate schemes. In England, too, where immediatism was also gaining followers, the general public had remained unmoved by gradualist proposals. Demands for "immediate, unconditional, uncompensated emancipation" thus appealed to young American idealists—at least the slogan was free of moral qualifications. Indeed, in 1831 the British government, responding to immediatist demands, enacted a massive program of gradual, compensated emancipation in the West Indies. But, even more important, by dedicating themselves to immediatism, the young reformers performed acts of self-liberation akin to the experience of conversion.

By freeing themselves from the shackles of gradualism, American abolitionists had finally triumphed over their feelings of selfishness, unworthiness, and alienation. Now they were morally fit to take God's side in the struggle against all the worldliness, license, cruelty, and selfishness that slaveowning had come to embody. Immediatists sensed themselves involved in a cosmic drama, a righteous war to redeem a fallen nation. They now felt ready to make supreme sacrifices and prove their fitness in their new religion of antislavery. "Never were men called on to die in a holier cause," wrote Amos A. Phelps in 1835 as he began his first tour as an abolitionist lecturer. It was far better, he thought, to die "as the negro's plighted friend" than to "sit in silken security, the consentor to & abettor of the manstealer's sin."

The campaign for Protestant reassertion had thus brought forth a vibrant romantic radicalism. Orthodox evangelicals quite rightly recoiled in fear. Abolitionists now put their faith entirely in the individual's ability to recognize and redeem himself from sin. No stifling traditions, no restrictive loyalties to institutions, no timorous concern for moderation or self-interest should be allowed to inhibit the free reign of Christian conscience. In its fullest sense, the phrase "immediate emancipation" described a transformed state of mind dominated by God and wholly at war with slavery. "The doctrine," wrote Elizur Wright, Jr., in 1833, "may be thus briefly stated":

> It is the duty of the holders of slaves to restore them to their liberty, and to extend to them the full protection of the law . . . to restore to them the profits of their labors, . . . to employ them as voluntary laborers on equitable wages. Also it is the *duty* of all men . . . to proclaim this doctrine, to urge upon slaveholders *immediate emancipation,* so long as there is a slave—to agitate the consciences of tyrants, so long as there is a tyrant on the globe.

Embedded in this statement was a vision of a new America, a daring affirmation that people of both races could reestablish their relationships on the basis of justice and Christian brotherhood. Like many other Americans who took up the burdens of reform, abolitionists envisioned their cause as leading to a society reborn in Christian brotherhood. Emancipation, like temperance, women's rights and communitarianism, became synonymous with the redemption of mankind and the opening of a purer phase of human history.

Abolitionists constantly tried to explain that they were not expecting some sudden Day of Jubilee when, with a shudder of collective remorse, the entire planter class would abruptly strike the shackles from all two million slaves and beg their forgiveness. Emancipation, they expected, would be achieved gradually; still it must be immediately begun. Immediatists were also forced to rebut the recurring charge that their demands promoted emancipation by rebellion on the plantations. "Our objects are to save life, not destroy it," Garrison exclaimed in 1831. "Make the slave free and every inducement to revolt is taken away." Few Americans believed these disclaimers. Instead, most suspected that immediate emancipation would suddenly create a large and mobile free population of inferior blacks. Most in the North were quite content to discriminate harshly against their black neighbors while the slaves remained at a safe distance on far-away plantations. According to Alexis de Tocqueville, the unusually acute foreign observer of antebellum society of the early 1830's: "Race prejudice seems stronger in those states that have abolished slavery than in those where it still exists, and nowhere is it more intolerant than in those states where it has never been known." White supremacy and support for slavery were thus inextricably bound up with all phases of American political, economic, and religious life.

Immediatist agitation was bound to provoke hostility from nearly every part of the social order.

As we have seen, by the 1830's the Northeast and Midwest enjoyed a thriving trade with the South, and the nation's economic well-being had become firmly tied to slave labor. Powerful financial considerations could thus dictate that abolitionism be harshly suppressed. Religious denominations were also deeply enmeshed in slavery, for Southerners were influential among the Methodists, Presbyterians, Anglicans, and Baptists. Little wonder that most clergymen vigorously rejected demands that their churches declare slaveholders in shocking violation of God's Law.

But by far the most consistent opponents of the abolitionist crusade were found in politics. Young reformers had long ago come to abhor what they saw as the hollow demagoguery and secularism of Jacksonian mass politics. By 1830 they were fully justified in adding the politician's unstinting support of slavery to their bill of particulars. As Richard H. Brown has shown, Jackson's Democratic Party was deliberately designed to uphold the planters' interests. Jacksonian ideology soon became synonymous with racism and anti-abolition. In the North, men who aspired to careers in Democratic Party politics had to solicit the approval of slaveholding party chiefs like Amos Kendall, John C. Calhoun, and Jackson himself. When anti-Jacksonian dissidents finally coalesced into the Whig Party during the 1830's, they, too, relied upon this formula for getting votes and recruiting leaders. Obviously, neither party dared to alienate proslavery interests in the South or racist supporters in the North. Moreover, as the Missouri and Nullification controversies had shown, political debates about slavery caused party allegiances to break ominously along sectional lines. For these reasons, party loyalty meant the suppression of all discussions of slavery.

The challenges which the abolitionists faced as they began their crusade were thus enormous. So was their own capability for disruption, although they were hardly aware of it at first. The ending of slavery whether peacefully or violently would require great changes in American life. Yet, if immediate emancipation provoked fear and violent hostility, it was nevertheless a doctrine appropriate to the age. The evangelical outlook with its rejection of tradition and expedience both embodied and challenged the culture that had created it. In retrospect, moderate approaches to the problem of slavery hardly seemed possible in Jacksonian America.

As a result, immediatist goals were anything but limited. Abolitionists now proposed to transform hundreds of millions of dollars worth of slaves into millions of black citizens by eradicating two centuries of American racism. Nevertheless, they sincerely felt that they promoted a conservative enterprise, and in certain respects this was an understandable (if misleading) self-assessment. Their unqualified attacks on slavery were, as they understood them, simply emulations of well-established evangelical methods. The Temperance Society's assault on liquor and the revivalist's denunciation of unbelief had hardly been characterized by restraint. Besides, immediatists were simply proposing an ideal by which all Christians were to measure themselves. They were not planning bloody revolution. They relied solely on voluntary conversion and rejected violence. As agitators, they defined their task as restoring time-honored American freedoms to an unjustly deprived people. Except for their opposition to racism, they offered no criticism of ordinary Protestant values. Was it anarchy, they wondered, to urge that pure Christian morality replace what they believed was the sexual abandon of the slave quarters? "Are we then fanatics," Garrison asked, "because we cry, *Do not rob! Do not murder!?* "

In their own eyes, then, abolitionists were hardly behaving like incendiaries as they opened their crusade. In slaveholding they discovered the ultimate source of the moral collapse which so deeply disturbed them. The race violence of Nat Turner and the secession threats of the "Nullifiers" constituted evidence that the nation had jettisoned all her moral ballasts. But immediate abolition seemed to hold forth the promise of Christian reconciliation between races, sections, and individuals. All motive for race revolt, all reason for political strife, and all inducement for moral degeneracy would be swept away. Indeed, the alternative of silence only invited the further spread of anarchy in a nation which Garrison described in 1831 as already "full of the blood of innocent men, women and babies—full of adultery and concupiscence—full of blasphemy, darkness and woeful rebellion against God—full of wounds and bruises and putrefying sores." Abolitionists were thus filled "with burning earnestness" when they insisted, as Elizur Wright did, that "the instant abolition of the whole slave system is safe." Most other Americans remained firm in their suspicions to the contrary.

Nevertheless, the abolitionists launched their crusade on a note of glowing optimism. Armed with moral certitude, they were also completely naïve politically. "The whole system of slavery will fall to pieces with a rapidity which will astonish," wrote Samuel E. Sewall, one of the first adherents to immediatism. Weld predicted in 1834 that complete equality for all blacks in the upper South was but two years away, and that "scores of clergymen in the slaveholding states . . . *are really with us.*" Anxious for the millennium, abolitionists had wholly misjudged the depth of

Northern racism, not to mention the extent of Southern tolerance.

All the same, there was wisdom in the naïveté. Without this romantic faith that God would put all things right, abolitionists would have lacked the incentive and creative stamina necessary for sustained assaults against slavery. Moreover, by stressing intuition as a sure guide to reality, abolitionists made an unprecedented attempt to establish empathy with the slave. One result, to be sure, was racist sentimentalism, a not surprising outcome considering the gulf which separated a Mississippi field hand from an independently wealthy Boston abolitionist. Yet the abolitionists were trying hard to imagine what it was like to be stripped of one's autonomy, prevented from protecting one's family, and deprived of legal safeguards and the rewards of one's own labor. This view of slavery made piecemeal reform completely unacceptable. To give slaves better food, fewer whippings, and some education was not enough. They deserved immediate justice, not charity. So convinced, and certain of ultimate victory, abolitionists set out to induce each American citizen to repent the sin of slavery.

3

Mobs and Martyrs:
The Dynamics of Moral Suasion

In December 1833, sixty-two abolitionists gathered in Philadelphia to form the American Anti-Slavery Society, a national organization devoted exclusively to promoting immediate emancipation. The meeting was well timed. Just six months earlier, in response to immediatist pressure in England, the British Parliament had enacted bills of emancipation for all slaves in the West Indies, an example which Northern humanitarians now felt inspired to emulate. Moreover, British reformers were once again involving themselves in American abolitionism, and this transatlantic cooperation was to remain a significant force in the antebellum era.

Most of all, the assembly represented a useful cross-section of those who were to lead the abolitionist crusade during the next three decades. Wealthy Lewis Tappan, for instance, spoke for socially respectable, wholly committed New York evangelicals, including his brother Arthur, jurist William Jay, and editor Joshua Leavitt. James G. Birney, Amos A. Phelps, Henry Brewster Stanton, Elizur Wright, Jr., Theodore D. Weld, and other evangelicals based in northeastern Ohio and upstate New York also identified strongly with the Tappans. William Lloyd Garrison headed a heterogeneous delegation of New England Congregation-alists like Samuel E. Sewall, Unitarians like Samuel J. May, and Quakers like John Greenleaf Whittier. Quakers ac-counted for twenty-one of the sixty-two in attendance. Four women (all Quakers) and three black men also signed the Society's Declaration of Sentiments, a foreshadowing of the significant contributions both groups were to make to the abolitionist cause. Racially mixed and eager to attract the assistance of women, the American Anti-Slavery Society was nonetheless controlled at its inception by talented and aggressive white men who combined religious zeal with aspirations as editors, businessmen, clerics, and philanthro-pists.

Garrison dominated the proceedings. Since January 1831 his newspaper, the *Liberator*, published in Boston, had been gaining notoriety for its resounding attacks on colonization and its advocacy of immediate, uncompensated emancipa-tion. Garrison's support among black activists in the North and especially in Boston had been growing ever since 1829, when he had first denounced gradualism in the columns of Benjamin Lundy's newspaper, the *Genius of Universal Emancipation.* It was Garrison who composed the American Anti-Slavery Society's Declaration of Sentiments.

In demanding immediate emancipation, Garrison's docu-ment explicitly endorsed nonviolence and firmly rejected "the use of all carnal weapons" by abolitionists and slaves; Christian principle forbade "the doing of evil that good may come." Harking back to the American Revolution, the Declaration noted that the colonists had "spilled human blood like water" while securing their own freedom, yet the patriots' grievances were "trifling" in comparison to those of the slave: "Our fathers were never slaves—never bought and sold like cattle—never shut out from the light of knowledge and religion—never subjected to the lash of brutal taskmasters." For citizens who enjoyed America's unique civil and religious liberty, toleration of slavery amounted to a personal sin "unequalled by any other on the face of the earth."

Abolitionists, therefore, were obliged to declare their unshakable opposition to colonization, to compensated emancipation, and to all laws upholding slavery. The slaves had every moral right to instant freedom and to the equal protection of the law; the bondsmen, not the slaveholders, deserved compensation. Every slaveowner was proven by Scripture to be a "MANSTEALER," for he had dared to "usurp the prerogative of Jehovah" by violating another's inalienable right to liberty. Finally, in what was clearly the most difficult portion of the Declaration to live up to, the signers pledged to oppose all racial prejudice wherever it appeared. Abolitionists must, as Garrison put it, "secure to the colored population . . . all the rights and privileges that belong to them as men and as Americans . . . The paths of preferment, of wealth, and of intelligence should be opened as widely to them as to persons of white complexion."

The Declaration appeared to most Americans as undiluted fanaticism. Yet the signers were pledging to act in ways which both reflected and greatly intensified some of the dominant social and economic trends of the era. In asserting that every person, regardless of race, should be "secure in his right to his own body—to the products of his own labor—to the protections of the law—to the common advantages of society," the Declaration affirmed with hitherto unparalleled force a set of social values to which many other Americans subscribed. Indeed, the call for immediate emancipation reflected a fervent desire to extend the tenets of economic self-reliance which, especially in the

North, were already transforming America into a nation devoted to individualistic capitalism.

Ironically, immediatists now found themselves insisting on values which had thrust the nation away from the orderly agricultural provincialism of their parents' time. Like their most consistent opponents in politics, the Jacksonians, abolitionist spokesmen affirmed that every individual had the inalienable right to advance by his own efforts. The good society, both groups believed, should tolerate no institutions which impeded a person's freedom to compete. In this sense, the Declaration of Sentiments reflected the same spirit which inspired Jacksonian assaults on "artificial" monopolies, the anti-Mason's call for the abolition of secret social clubs, and the nativists' warnings about the Catholic hierarchy's "unnatural influence."

But here the similarities ended. Members of the American Anti-Slavery Society could hardly condone the Jacksonians' racism, their acceptance of local diversity, their pandering to public opinion. As they dismantled the National Bank, Jacksonian Democrats explained that they were simply restoring economic freedom to the common people. Citizens could now invest as they wished—in a slave or a candy store, it made no difference. To the abolitionists, of course, it made quite literally all the difference in the world.

Immediatism thus contained a vision of competitive society hitherto unparalleled in its inclusiveness. After emancipation, vocational independence, Biblical morality, family autonomy, unimpeded mobility, and republican governance were to reign supreme. Blacks in both sections of the country were to be fully included in the new Christian era. Slaves, their former masters, and liberated poor whites would all exercise their God-given rights to improve themselves, unhampered by the tyranny of race exploitation. The planters' sterile fields, producing now "but half a crop," would soon "smile beneath the plow of the freeman, the genial influence of just and equitable wages," as Elizur Wright, Jr., put it. The Mason-Dixon line, the segregated school, would give way to a homogeneous America in which, as Garrison wrote in 1831, "black skin will not be merely endurable, but *popular*." The trumpet call of "immediate emancipation" thus portended the eventual emergence of America's modern capitalist order. In this most fundamental sense, abolitionists were indeed what they saw themselves to be—the prophets of a new age.

The Philadelphia delegates performed their prophetic roles with great seriousness. According to the Declaration, members of the American Anti-Slavery Society pledged to begin organizing antislavery societies in every town, city, and village. The Society would also circulate antislavery tracts and newspapers, aiming to convert ministers and editors, men with direct influence over public opinion. Abolitionists hoped to purify the churches in particular. If clergymen endorsed immediatism and preached from Southern pulpits the sin of slaveholding, planters would be moved, for the sake of their souls, to release their bondsmen. The slaveholder, the Negro-hater, and the apathetic citizen were certain to repent, just as each abolitionist himself had repented his sinful complicity with oppression. The "dam of prejudice" would give way, unleashing "one still, deep, rapid, mighty current" of conversion, contrition, and emancipation. "Oh," rhapsodized Elizur Wright, Jr., in 1833, "how it will sweep away those refuges of lies!" Prejudice and slaveowning, outward manifestations of unregenerate hearts, were thus to be conquered with the tools of revivalism: "moral suasion," as immediatists referred to it. This is what the Declaration meant when it dedicated the American Anti-Slavery Society to "the destruction of error by the potency of truth—the overthrow of prejudice by the power of love—and the abolition of slavery by the spirit of repentance."

Having made these commitments, abolitionists almost naturally turned upon the American Colonization Society. They realized from the outset that to be effective, their demand for immediate emancipation had to be free of equivocation. From the first they resisted all challenges to put forward "practical" schemes for easing the slaves' transition to freedom. "Practicality" thus dictated compromise, and abolitionists rejected it in all forms, especially that of colonization. All such discussion, they felt, deflected attention from society's fundamental problems—white racism and Negro enslavement. Until whites had accepted blacks as equals, digressions on practical alternatives to immediatism would only reinforce prejudice and encourage complacency. This was what Garrison meant by his comment that "the genius of the abolition movement is to have *no plan.*"

In April 1831, an editorial by Garrison in the *Liberator* boldly proclaimed that the Colonization Society constituted a *"conspiracy against human rights"* which had to be crushed if the nation was to purge itself of sinful prejudice. After the founding of the New England Anti-Slavery Society in 1832, abolitionist agents began organizing anticolonization rallies in Massachusetts, Connecticut, Vermont, and New Hampshire. That same year, with funding supplied by Arthur Tappan, Garrison published his *Thoughts on African Colonization*, an unwieldy compendium made up in part of racist quotations from leading colonizationists. Garrison also included extended statements from black spokesmen which demonstrated their unremitting hostility to emigration. From then on, intermittent pamphlet warfare between colonizationists and immediatists became a permanent feature of the antebellum decades.

For the young abolitionists, these were indeed exhilarating, fulfilling times. As they battled the colonizationists and initiated their first moral-suasion projects, they felt themselves bound together in holy association of selfless and kindred spirits. Fifty years afterward, Lydia Maria Child recalled with nostalgia that "mortals were never more sublimely forgetful of self" than were the antislavery men and women of the 1830's. "How quick the 'mingled flute and trumpet eloquence' of [Wendell] Phillips responded to the clarion-call of Garrison . . . How wealth poured in from the ever open hands of Arthur Tappan, Gerrit Smith, and thousands of others." Such feelings seemed almost sufficient recompense for pleading the slave's cause. Certainly, the spirit of brotherhood and sisterhood which suffused the abolitionists' letters to one another suggested that the reformers drew satisfying contrasts between their circles of spontaneity and love, and the pretense, selfishness, and racism of the "unredeemed" world. The importance of such psychological rewards is hard to overestimate. Especially during the 1830's, abolitionists seldom enjoyed a clearcut victory over the forces which upheld slavery.

One dramatic exception, however, was the successful 1834 student rebellion at Cincinnati's Lane Seminary. In Theodore Weld the Cincinnati drama was furnished with an arresting central character. A protegé of Charles G. Finney, Weld had served in 1831 as a preceptor at the Oneida Institute, a manual-labor school in western New York. A center of evangelical activity, the institute was soon to become a hive of abolitionism as well under the presidency of immediatist Beriah Green. The school enjoyed the patronage of Lewis Tappan, who sent his sons there, and in the process Tappan became Weld's close friend and religious confidant. A restless, moody man, Weld could also suddenly radiate a spontaneous Christian compassion and charisma which associates found irresistible. Here was just the man, thought the Tappans in early 1834, to extend moral suasion and Christian benevolence to the unruly frontier.

Arthur Tappan had already invested heavily in an Ohio reform project, Lane Seminary, which had been established by New York evangelicals as an outpost of revivalism in Cincinnati. Lyman Beecher, one of New England's most august evangelical ministers, had already agreed to leave Boston and assume Lane's presidency. Now resolving to make the seminary a citadel of Yankee abolitionism, the Tappans dispatched Weld to Cincinnati in early 1834, and results were not long in coming. Weld took with him Oneida students like Henry B. Stanton who were already well-schooled in the formulas of immediatism. Others, likewise destined for leadership in abolition, also converged on the seminary, attracted by an admissions policy which encouraged "people of color" to apply. Under Weld's direction, the students at once initiated public discussions on the merits of immediate emancipation.

Eighteen days later, after prayerful evenings and "protracted sessions," the students and faculty endorsed immediatism and vowed their implacable opposition to colonization. "The Lord has done great things for us here," Weld reported to Lewis Tappan. "Eight months ago there was not an immediate abolitionist in this seminary . . . and abolitionism was regarded as the climax of absurdity, fanaticism and blood." Thus displayed, in all their purity, were the fruits of moral suasion. After organizing an antislavery society, the students affirmed their liberation from prejudice by working to spread literacy and piety within the local black community. Augustus Wattles and Marius Robinson even suspended their studies for a year of full-time service in a black elementary school.

Cincinnati's white citizens, some of whom had only four years earlier turned viciously against their black neighbors in bloody riot, were incensed. The worried trustees, in turn, ordered students and faculty to disband their antislavery society. President Beecher assured Lewis Tappan of his commitment to "free discussion," but could effect no compromise between the trustees and the rebels. Forty students led by Weld thereupon renounced their affiliation with the seminary and pursued their activities in Cincinnati with even greater zeal. Abolitionists had turned upon their evangelical fathers. In Lyman Beecher's case, the rebellion entered his own family. Only Catherine, his eldest daughter, supported her father's efforts at compromise. Harriet Beecher expressed her entire sympathy with the seceding students. She was not yet married to Lane's Professor of Biblical Literature, Calvin Stowe.

Ultimately the Lane rebels found a congenial home in Oberlin, a small town in northwest Ohio, and once again the Tappans supplied initial funding for a new college. For the first time in the history of higher education, instruction was open equally to men, women, and blacks, and "free discussion" was upheld in the college charter. Charles G. Finney joined the faculty, but Weld declined a professorship in theology, preferring to evangelize the countryside against slavery. Still, he retained close ties with Oberlin, which soon became the hub of Western abolitionism and the nation's finest example of integrated learning. Throughout the 1830's Weld and his associates lectured and passed out tracts to spread the message of abolition in hundreds of Ohio and upstate New York communities.

During these first years of agitation, even Southern whites occasionally found themselves submitting to the logic of immediatism. To abolitionists the repentant slaveholder was a most valuable source of antislavery testimony. Southern-born crusaders such as Marius Robinson and James G. Birney bore authentic witness to slavery's sinfulness. These adherents also seemed to confirm the abolitionists' expectation that Southern whites could be won over. "I read with tears of joy and gratitude!" exclaimed Lewis Tappan in 1835 after learning of Birney's conversion.

Southern immediatists were anomalies, however, not harbingers of repentance in the slave states. Although coming from slaveholding families, Southerners like Birney, Angelina Grimké (who later married Theodore D. Weld), and Sarah M. Grimké had experienced upbringings which had departed significantly from plantation norms. Birney's Presbyterian father, for example, was the wealthiest, most prestigious slaveowner in Danville, Kentucky. Because of his unquestioned community standing, he took the lead in evangelical projects which his lesser neighbors whispered were dangerously close to New England ways. While promoting a decidedly antislavery form of colonization and supporting temperance, the Tract Society, and the Sunday School Union, the elder Birney had also insisted on a sound Yankee education at Princéton for his son. Such a background set young James Birney on a course which began with colonization and ended with uncompromising immediatism. Another plantation-bred abolitionist, William T. Allan, was raised by a Presbyterian minister who felt no misgivings about inviting Theodore Weld to his Huntsville, Alabama, residence to discuss abolitionism. Soon after their discussion, Dr. Allan enrolled his son in Lane Seminary. William T. Allan was to become president of the student antislavery society. Clearly, these were not the children of typical plantation families.

Neither were other recruits who had been raised in parts of the upper South. In these older border areas and in more recently settled parts of eastern Tennessee, central Kentucky and northern Missouri, slavery had given way to a more commercial economy and culture. Here Quakers, Moravians, and free-will Baptists often exhibited decided preferences for commercial careers, evangelicalism, and benevolent activity. During the 1820's these people had constituted practically all the Southern support for Benjamin Lundy's gradualist programs. In places like Jonesboro, Tennessee, and Guilford, North Carolina, the pious citizenry fretted over the free blacks, observed their temperance vows, supported missionaries, and endorsed a range of benevolent projects. Farther south, however, the traditions of plantation society held sway. Here nonslaveowning whites and planters alike fiercely resisted all such evangelical impulses, fearing quite correctly for the safety of their local traditions and white hegemony. In the context of authentic slaveowning society, Birney was ultimately no less an alien than was Garrison or Lewis Tappan.

Yet Birney's Southern origins furnished him with an important conclusion, one which at first eluded his Northern-bred colleagues. The "slaveholder's tenacity" made him "perfectly at ease in his iniquity," Birney warned in 1835. The prospects of converting him were indeed small, and "repentance is far off." Southerners in turn were busy giving substance to Birney's observation. In 1831, in the wake of David Walker's *Appeal* and the Nat Turner insurrection, town meetings throughout the South put up rewards for the apprehension of persons caught circulating abolitionist literature. In South Carolina, Governor James Hamilton, Jr., and Senator Robert Y. Hayne attempted to enlist the mayor of Boston in efforts to silence Garrison; Georgia's legislature appropriated five thousand dollars to reward the daring soul who would seize the Boston editor and bring him South for trial. And during the summer of 1835 a young Lane student named Amos Dresser arrived in Nashville, Tennessee, ostensibly to sell Bibles for his next year's tuition. He also planned to promote immediatism in his spare time, but someone discovered his supply of abolitionist literature. Charged as an antislavery agent, he was tried by a vigilance committee and publicly given twenty lashings while a large, cheering crowd looked on. He was fortunate to have been let off so lightly.

In retrospect, such hostility hardly seems surprising. Even before the rise of immediatism, many planters had concluded that serious discussions of slavery were too subversive to be permitted. Aggressive justifications of the institution as a positive good had, in fact, predated by more than a decade the appearance of the *Liberator*. And, after the violent events of 1831, Southern whites became even more sensitive to the dangers of agitation. Responding in part to the Turner revolt and to the continuing presence of so many free blacks, the Virginia legislature had opened a fateful debate on a gradual emancipation bill. Masters were to be compensated and all blacks expelled. Supported largely by freehold farmers and frontiersmen from back-country western Virginia (after 1861 the unionist state of West Virginia), the bill was decisively defeated. The vote signaled the collapse of all forthright discussions of slavery. Proslavery forces from then on enjoyed supremacy throughout the South. All chance of abolitionist negotiation with moderate slaveholders (if, indeed, there had ever been any) vanished.

Opposition to abolitionism from Northerners was equally predictable. Because slavery had become by the 1830's interwoven with nearly all American institutions, Northern politicians, ministers, and businessmen all could find ample motives for opposing the immediatists. Race prejudice also continued to permeate white culture in the North. In the

ever-shifting, confusing circumstances of this rapidly expanding region, white skin became an increasingly compelling assurance of stable identity.

Racial solidarity among whites served to mute otherwise
dangerous class antagonism in both the North and the
South. Regardless of the obvious gulf between rich and poor
which often characterized Jacksonian America, especially in
the South and in the cities, all Caucasians could enjoy the
fraternity of white skin. From this perspective, the unskilled
worker on the Boston docks could sense his equality with
the Winthrops and Adamses; the back-country Virginia
"cracker" could measure himself with confidence against
the Lees. Finally, by attacking the Colonization Society,
immediatists quickly provoked hostility from some of the
nation's most influential citizens, who now withdrew their
own criticisms of slavery to voice instead their opposition to
"fanatical Garrisonism."

At first, Northern intransigence focused on thwarting the
abolitionists' efforts to aid local blacks. But such opposition
only made abolitionists more certain that they must wage
war simultaneously against racism in the nation and slavery
in the South. Bondage could never be ended, abolitionists
reasoned, if negrophobic attitudes always inhibited others
from taking a genuine interest in their crusade. Hoping to
dissipate racism, white abolitionists tried a number of
techniques. Quoting the Bible, they emphasized that God
had made *all* men in His image, not just the whites.
Appealing to history, they pointed to figures like Hannibal,
Alexandre Dumas, Crispus Attucks, Saint Augustine, the
Egyptian Pharaohs, and others with reputedly dark skin. In
fugitive slaves like Frederick Douglass and in freeborn
blacks like Samuel Ringgold Ward, whites discovered black
people with superior skills and demeanor who wholly belied
the myth of innate inferiority. The oppressive environment

created by slavery and discrimination, abolitionists argued, produced the economic backwardness, intellectual dullness, and moral insensibility which whites so insistently claimed were the hallmarks of black American culture. As Lydia Maria Child once asserted, "In the United States, colored persons have scarcely any chance to rise. But if colored people are well treated, and have the same inducements to industry as others, they [will] work as well and behave as well." So convinced, white reformers also set about encouraging local self-help among Northern free blacks. By so doing they stimulated antiabolitionist fears which often led to acts of direct reprisal.

As noted, the white citizens of Cincinnati had not been kindly disposed to the Lane students' attempts to work with local blacks. Canterbury, Connecticut, in 1833 witnessed a more extreme form of protest, however, when Quaker schoolmistress Prudence Crandall decided to admit a black child to her private academy for girls. After incensed white parents had withdrawn their children, Crandall, at Garrison's suggestion, began to recruit an all-black student body. The townspeople then placed the school under an economic boycott, poisoned Crandall's well with animal feces, and lobbied successfully for a state law which made operating such a school illegal. Crandall defied the law, and spent a number of months in jail. Upon her release in 1834 she announced that classes would resume. Canterbury's citizens thereupon assembled, attacked the building with crowbars, and tried to set it on fire. The school never reopened, but in 1838 the Connecticut legislature did repeal the law which had thwarted Crandall's experiment in black education. In Canaan, New Hampshire, the townsfolk resorted to speedier methods. Discovering that abolitionists were planning to open an integrated academy, they obtained a brace of draft horses and dragged the building into a swamp. In light of such experiences, there was great merit in the view that the whites, not the blacks, were the ones most needing cultural uplift. After passing through even more harrowing experiences with mob violence which lay ahead, most antislavery reformers found it hard to disagree.

From the late 1820's to the late 1830's, Americans witnessed outbursts of civil disorder unparalleled in their national history. Mobs, riots, and lynchings suddenly erupted everywhere—in cities, in the countryside, in the North as well as the South. By 1834, angry citizens had already attacked Catholic convents in upstate New York, looted the homes of Baltimore bankers, fired the dwellings of blacks in Philadelphia and Boston, and disrupted a number of Masonic meetings. So commonplace had violence become that at times, especially after 1834, there arose in some quarters a fear of total social disintegration. In 1834 abolitionists had discovered that they, too, had become the targets of mob action.

The tenor of Jacksonian society invited Americans to vigilantism. By the mid-1830's riotous behavior had become an accepted way of addressing society's religious, ethnic, and political tensions. As we have seen, the ethos of the period reemphasized the individual's primacy over artificial restrictions. Consequently, people sensed deeply the imperative to participate without restraint in the shaping of public life. Even Andrew Jackson projected an anarchic image. Here, it seemed, was a man who served democracy best when he trusted his instincts and took the law unto himself when abolishing banks and defying courts. Thus inspired, many antebellum Americans came to believe, as David Grimsted has explained, "that man standing above the law was not to be a threat to society, but its fulfillment." Legal procedures could be ignored as a tangle of traditions which the wealthy and unscrupulous manipulated for their own ends.

Yet those who participated in riotous action were hardly anarchists. Like the defenders of riots in general, antiabolitionists denied with sincere vehemence that their disruptions subverted the social order. To the contrary, they explained that they were acting quickly to preserve popular rule by stopping insidious groups which duly appointed authorities were powerless to restrain. This, then, was the state of mind which stimulated the many riots of the 1830's and which influenced Northern foes of immediatism to take to the street.

But the antiabolitionist mobs arose from specific social causes as well. Leonard D. Richards has shown with exceptional research that as abolitionist activity became better funded and supported by more local societies, violent opposition also increased. In December 1831, when Garrison first began distributing the *Liberator*, his denunciations did not incite Bostonians to violence. Nearly two years later, on October 2, 1833, fifteen hundred New Yorkers, the first large body of antiabolitionist rioters, stormed the Chatham Chapel looking for Garrison and Arthur Tappan. The background to this Chatham Chapel incident provides a good example of the interaction between abolitionist effort and mob violence.

During this two-year interval between 1831 and 1833, abolitionism had begun to make some gains. January 1832 had witnessed the formation of the New England Anti-Slavery Society and the start of campaigns to aid free blacks and to discredit the American Colonization Society. By late 1833, abolitionism had expanded from four local societies in two states to forty-seven in ten states. In far-off Hudson, Ohio, Elizur Wright, Jr., was quoting Garrison's *Thoughts* in debates at Colonization Society meetings; in still further-off London, Garrison himself had captured the cash subsidies of English abolitionists, much to the colonizationists' dismay. Back in New York, this same year, Arthur Tappan stunned the colonizationists further by throwing his immense wealth behind Garrison. Meanwhile, contributions to their own cause plummeted as with a wrenching suddenness, they sensed themselves under siege by a tightly organized, well-funded, and far-flung network of Anglo-American enemies. Fearing unspeakable transformations of the white social order, the New York mob, led by colonizationists, began to assemble in October 1833.

Members of antiabolitionist mobs did indeed believe that the entire social fabric was under heavy attack by the "friends of the slave." As Richards has also explained, antiabolitionists for the most part represented the North's older provincial elites. Usually led by prominent lawyers, doctors, judges, and congressmen, most mobs were composed largely of high-ranking professionals and men involved in local business. Abolitionists referred to them with disdain and accuracy as "gentlemen of property and standing." In an age of growing commercialization and regional interdependence, such persons depended for their status and livelihood on the local economy of a rapidly passing era. Many were middle-aged, well-settled descendants of distinguished New England families. Usually their status also depended on their leadership in traditional organizations such as the Episcopal Church, the "old school" (antievangelical) Presbyterian Church, and the local Colonization Society. Many antiabolitionists also had strong roots in local political juntos, regarding themselves as "zealous" Whigs or Democrats.

Little wonder that such persons feared abolitionism as a highly developed effort by meddlesome outsiders to undermine their authority. They shuddered at the thought of a movement organized from afar by faceless, wealthy men, which suddenly and without invitation began intervening in their neighborhood affairs. The tactics of moral suasion, as we have seen, were designed to appeal directly to all persons—men, women, and children alike, paying no heed to local leadership.

Abolitionist ideology did indeed emphasize moral homogeneity, economic individualism, and social cosmopolitanism—forces which undercut patriarchy and traditional deference. Moreover, recent research indicates that the rank-and-file abolitionists were a broad-based group which was gaining in status during this age of economic growth. While their opponents were led by local squires, most abolitionists came from less distinguished Protestant stock. Indeed, some immediatists must have seemed to their opponents like rootless outsiders, for recently emigrated Englishmen were often attracted to the movement. In religion, of course, the abolitionists' evangelicalism stood in sharp contrast to the sacramental elitism of their foes. Occupationally, rank-and-file abolitionists seemed to be far more versatile (if less wealthy) than the "gentlemen of property and standing." The abolitionists included a high percentage of farmers, manufacturers, tradesmen, and artisans. Unlike the high-ranking rioters, abolitionists often pursued careers which required broadly applicable skills and put little stress on traditionally determined local status. As we shall see in Chapter 4, it was no accident that Northern strongholds of antislavery feeling were also rural areas which had successfully come to terms with the new cosmopolitan economy. In the abolitionists' threats to their time-honored hegemony, elite Yankee provincials thus discovered their profound commonality with the fiercely localistic planters and poor whites of the slave states. Upon so doing, they took to the streets. In the 1850's, during sporadic renewals of antiabolitionist violence, Irish Catholic immigrants once again demonstrated these concerns. These Irish were hardly moved by the glories of Federalism or the beauties of the plantation, but they, like the bluestocking Yankee and the plantation nabob, were wholly dedicated to protecting their own particular and clannish ways.

During the mid-1830's the enemies of abolitionism had ample reason for believing that the movement was becoming ever more formidable and far-flung. By the end of 1834, in New York City, people of great financial power and expertise had taken control of the American Anti-Slavery Society. Wealthy immediatists like the Tappan brothers and Gerrit Smith contributed vast fortunes to underwrite abolitionism. Lewis Tappan, Joshua Leavitt, and especially the Society's Corresponding Secretary, Elizur Wright, Jr., commanded bureaucratic skills exceptional in any era. They commissioned, paid, and equipped the many agents who organized local societies throughout the North. Soon, antislavery societies did begin to spring up; to the consternation of the local squires, these cells not only pressed ahead with agitation but served as efficient auxiliaries of the remote but seemingly all-powerful parent body in New York City.

Opponents also grew more vocal as abolitionists expanded their journalistic efforts. By 1834 the *Liberator*, always under Garrison's sole jurisdiction, had been joined by a battery of new publications. Abolitionists were now plunging wholeheartedly into the field of mass communications. The *Emancipator*, published in New York, aimed for national circulation and spoke officially for the parent society. By 1836 in Cincinnati, James G. Birney had braved mob assaults as he struggled to get out copies of his weekly *Philanthropist*. The flow of illustrated periodicals bearing titles like *Anti-Slavery Reporter, Slave's Friend* (for juvenile readers), and *Human Rights* suddenly seemed endless. Talented polemicists like Lydia Maria Child, Angelina Grimké, William Jay, Elizur Wright, Jr., and Amos A. Phelps also availed themselves of the steam-driven press, publishing their own compelling appeals against slavery. In May 1835, as a culmination of all these endeavors, the American Anti-Slavery Society embarked on a new project. Its aim, as Lewis Tappan put it, was "to sow the good seed of abolition thoroughly over the whole country," to flood every town and hamlet, North and South, with mailings of abolitionist literature. "The great postal campaign," as the abolitionists referred to it, set off a momentous reaction of mob activity in the North, repression in the South, and controversy in Congress. At the same time, this daring endeavor and the uproar it provoked also began to draw many people, hitherto uncommitted, to adopt antislavery positions.

With an initial budget of thirty thousand dollars, the postal campaign turned out to be a pamphleteering effort of unprecedented proportions. Ministers, elected officials, and newspaper editors in every state, but especially in the South, were placed on the mailing lists. Slaves and Southern free blacks, contrary to antiabolitionist charges, were not. One-by-one, life-long slaveholders would begin to repent, the abolitionists expected. World opinion, masters would realize, was "a feeling against which they cannot stand." After freeing their slaves, these Southern manumissionists would then add their rebukes against those who continued, as Elizur Wright, Jr., put it, to "ply the lash." Romantic and unrealistic as they were, these were the goals of the "great postal campaign." According to Bertram Wyatt-Brown, over 175,000 items were dispatched through the New York City post office in July 1835 alone. By the end of 1837, the

American Anti-Slavery Society had issued over a million pieces of antislavery literature. In the interval, hysteria swept through the South. Major Northern cities and small towns had witnessed riotous mobs. Northern state legislatures and even Congress had begun debating measures to curtail antislavery agitation. The number of antislavery societies in the North had also mushroomed. A failure when judged by its own goals, the postal campaign nevertheless transformed abolitionism into a subject that no American could ignore.

The Southern reaction, swift and severe, took the abolitionists aback. It also doomed their hopes of peacefully converting the slaveholder. Just after the mail from New York arrived, on July 29, 1835, angry South Carolinians broke into the Charleston post office and hauled away the satchels. The next evening, the mob reassembled and hung up effigies of Garrison and Arthur Tappan. These were then consumed by a bonfire of abolitionist newspapers which were ignited underneath them. Leading planters organized vigilance societies to search the incoming mail and confiscate "incendiary literature." "The indications are that the South is unanimous in their resistance," John C. Calhoun announced, correctly. Clerics and congressmen throughout the slave states thundered against depraved Yankee conspirators. Everywhere in the South, free blacks (feared as the chief targets of abolitionist plans for race war) faced ever more systematic repression, even reenslavement. President Andrew Jackson made known his approval of the white Southerners' behavior. In his Annual Message to Congress, circulated in December, Jackson decried the postal campaign and urged Congress to ban antislavery literature from the United States mails. Soon, several Southern state legislatures passed resolutions addressed to Northern state governments which called for laws to silence abolitionism. Connecticut responded with its famous 1836 "gag law" attempting to ban peripatetic abolitionist speakers. No other Northern legislature complied, but their own denunciations of abolitionism encouraged the "gentlemen of property and standing" to take action. So, undoubtedly, did the success of Southern resistance and the uninhibited antiabolitionist rhetoric of the President of the United States.

Autumn 1835 saw antiabolitionists all over the North creating violent uproar. Well-organized cadres of leading citizens began taking reprisals, usually directed at local gatherings of abolitionists and at the editors of antislavery newspapers. In a few instances mob violence arose spontaneously, as in New York City during 1834. Here, lower-class whites ran amuck in nearby black neighborhoods and also destroyed the property of white abolitionists. The far more typical antiabolitionist riot was planned in advance and led by the local elites. In the Utica riot of October 1835, the pillars of the community took the lead against outside agitators as lawyers, politicians, merchants, and bankers broke up a state convention of abolitionists and roughed up several delegates. The Cincinnati mobs which repeatedly attacked James G. Birney's press were similarly composed.

In New England, too, violence seemed pervasive. Lydia Maria Child, like other abolitionists, imagined herself passing through scenes like those "of the French Revolution, when no man dared trust his neighbors." As the British abolitionist George Thompson and Garrison made their way from meeting to meeting, mobs greeted them at nearly every stop. In Boston in October 1835, a mob looking for Thompson stumbled instead upon Garrison and dragged him through the streets. Outside New England, abolitionist agents fared no better. Henry B. Stanton, operating in Ohio and Pennsylvania, estimated that during this period he had faced mobs on more than seventy occasions.

But the most frightening scenes of all transpired in Alton, a small river town in extreme southern Illinois. In late 1837 the city's leaders finally lost all patience with Elijah P. Lovejoy, an interloper from Maine who edited the *Observer*, a newspaper equally uncompromising in its anti-Catholicism and antislavery. Local politicians, civil authorities, and other prominent citizens made clear their unwillingness to protect Lovejoy from harm. He and his supporters refused to be cowed, even after mobs had repeatedly thrown Lovejoy's printing presses into the river. On November 7, 1837, a mob again gathered, this time around the warehouse where Lovejoy and his adherents, armed, were guarding yet another press. They set the building afire. As Lovejoy rushed from the burning building, gun in hand, he was stopped by a bullet. Antiabolitionist violence, which had until now focused on destroying property, had finally culminated in public murder. Immediatism had found its first martyr.

The wave of terrorism finally subsided in 1838; it had produced ironic but highly significant results. Every attempt to silence the abolitionists only drew attention to the movement and publicized its principles. From the first, the abolitionists exploited this fact fully, transforming mob actions into vehicles for moral suasion. "How the heathen rage!" wrote an exultant Samuel J. May to Garrison during the height of the violence. "Our opposers are doing everything to help us." Never before, he thought, had any subject been "ever so much talked about as slavery is everywhere." Abolitionists marked with satisfaction the ringing debates on slavery in newspapers and legislatures which accompanied the censorship proposals and riot reports. "The cause *is* progressing," John Greenleaf Whittier decided. "I want no better evidence of it than the rabid violence of our enemies."

But even as abolitionists reassured one another about the benefits of repression, they also began to draw more sophisticated conclusions from their violent experiences. The pervasiveness of antiabolitionism certainly cast grave doubts upon their first perception of a nation ready to respond quickly to "truth." Mobs in the North and massive resistance in the South, moreover, put the lie to their vision that moral suasion would inaugurate a new era of national harmony and interracial brotherhood. In late 1837, Garrison expressed well the feeling of stunned frustration which had overtaken the entire movement as it abandoned its shattered first hopes for peace and national unity through abolition. "When we first unfurled the banner of the *Liberator*," he wrote, "we did not anticipate that, in order to protect southern slavery, the free states would voluntarily trample under foot all order, law and government, or brand the advocates of universal liberty as incendiaries." Judged by its own aims, moral suasion had failed utterly; yet the opposition it had provoked was opening new possibilities, suggesting new tactics and new goals. Discouraging as it was, repression nonetheless did make some genuine converts. More important, it was helping to create a broad constituency of antislavery sympathizers concerned with preserving civil liberties. By the late 1830's, none could deny that, despite their failures, the abolitionists were making slavery a central issue in American life.

4

Petitions, Perfectionists, and Political Abolitionists

Albert Gallatin Riddle, a seasoned though obscure antislavery activist in northern Ohio, was always ready to share his observations on local matters. Certainly he was well qualified to do so, counting among his friends influential sectional politicians and numerous Oberlin immediatists. During the Civil War he was to represent the Western Reserve in Congress, and he spent his final years writing perceptive essays on the history of abolitionism. In 1842 he reported to Joshua Giddings, his representative in Washington, that a "wide and deep feeling" of antagonism against the South "was silently stealing upon the hearts of our people." Mention "the question of Southern dictation, and you see their eyes flash." Here, immediatists agreed, was the most heartening result of the violent 1830's. By the end of the decade some of abolitionism's most important leaders had declared their "conversions," embarking on lifetime careers as immediatist agitators. But far more commonly, abolitionist agitation and the repressive efforts of its opponents had the combined effect of creating partially committed sympathizers, people like the ones Riddle described.

These important constituencies, concentrated within clear geographic boundaries, became centers for abolitionism and also the breeding grounds for sectional impulses in American politics. By 1840, 2.5 million black Southerners seemed no closer to freedom than they had been a decade earlier. Yet abolitionists could also note an ambiguous "progress" in some parts of the North.

The most dramatic and easy-to-document progress, of course, was the number of conversions. Mob actions, as it turned out, not only created sympathy for their victims but brought a number of important new people directly into the movement. Philanthropist Gerrit Smith, for example, had successfully resisted the combined moral suasion of Theodore D. Weld, Lewis Tappan, and James G. Birney. Then came the Utica riot, which took place near his Peterboro estate. Smith at once joined hands with the immediatists. Others like Dr. Henry Bowditch and Edmund Quincy dated their respective conversions to the mobbing of Garrison and the murder of Lovejoy. Yet it is clear, contrary to the oft-repeated assertion of some historians, that violent events provided only the occasions for these commitments and were not the causes. Most Americans who witnessed the mobs left without displaying even the remotest signs of concern.

In most cases, those converted by the mobs had already demonstrated an interest in reform. More important, they had also shown some signs of a major refocusing of values. Wendell Phillips, for example, was blessed with wealth, a keen mind, rhetorical brilliance, striking good looks, and two degrees from Harvard. Expected to join the Winthrops and Lawrences in Massachusetts' Whig elite, he displayed no enthusiasm for his glowing prospects as he haphazardly practiced law during the mid-1830's. Witnessing the 1835 Garrison mob in Boston, Phillips felt disturbed, but was "puzzled rather than astounded," as he recalled years later. He remained uncommitted ("I did not understand antislavery then") and remained on the fringes of the legal establishment and the local abolitionist societies. By late 1837, however, he had already defied his mother by impulsively marrying the brilliant but chronically infirm Ann Terry Greene, an abolitionist, to whom he had proposed on what all mistakenly had agreed was her deathbed. In the context of this emotional upheaval, Phillips heard the news of the Alton riots and his remaining indecision vanished. "The gun which was aimed at the breast of Lovejoy . . . brought me to my feet" is the way he described his reaction. For the rest of his life, Phillips put his voice and intellect behind abolitionism, women's rights, and other radical causes. Lovejoy's murder thus provided a catalyst for Phillips's conversion, but was hardly the reason for it.

Important as they were, commitments like Smith's and Phillips's shrink in significance when compared with the spread of strong antislavery attitudes throughout whole regions of the North. Again, antiabolitionist violence and Southern repression provided the catalyst. The disrupted meetings, the mail searches, the wrecked newspaper offices —above all, the murder of Lovejoy—began to make many Northerners, abolitionists and nonabolitionists alike, wonder about the safety of America's civil liberties. Many came increasingly to fear that slaveholders harbored contempt for the freedoms of all other Americans, black or white. Moreover, riots in Alton, Utica, Cincinnati, and elsewhere seemed to provide chilling documentation of the planter classes' ability to extend a relentless hegemony into the heart of the North. Dupes and pawns, the "gentlemen of property and standing" seemed ready to sacrifice the freedoms of their neighbors while serving the undemocratic interests of far-away slaveowning nabobs. This was the "slave-power conspiracy" to which Northerners increasingly referred in the years before the Civil War. As Birney once put it, "Whilst our aristocracy would preserve the domestic peace of the South, they seem totally to disregard the domestic peace of the North." Antislavery feeling in this sense resembled its opposite. Supporters as well as opponents of abolition grew more numerous as both movements generated fears of conspiracy, which then seemed confirmed by the course of events. Many who were not abolitionists began to suspect that repression was transforming American freedoms into "hollow counterfeits." "FREE!," Theodore Weld exploded upon hearing of Lovejoy's death. "The word and the sounds are omnipresent masks and mockers. An impious lie unless they stand for free *Lynch Law*, and free *murder*; for they *are* free."

For Northerners who felt as Weld did, concern for civil rights rapidly merged with a general endorsement of some of the abolitionists' fundamental principles. To be sure, many immediatists were careful to distinguish themselves, the "true" abolitionists, from those whites who cared for their own civil rights, but not for those of the slave. Historians have also found it convenient to make a rigorous distinction between such anti-Southern or antislavery feelings and the radical doctrines of immediate abolitionism. They contrast abolitionism as a coherent emancipationist movement with this less committed, less egalitarian opposition to slavery. While useful, the distinction can also be misleading, especially when assessing abolitionism's political impact. For one thing slaveholders never bothered with such fine discriminations. Moreover, many immediate abolitionists showed no less concern than other white Northerners about the fate of republican freedom in a nation which supported slaveowning. The idea that emancipation would salvage the liberties of *all* Americans was commonplace in immediatist literature. As Birney once put it: "The liberties of those yet free are in imminent peril . . . It is not only for the emancipation of the enslaved that we contend."

Immediatism was also difficult to separate from broader anti-Southern opinions, for these intertwining sentiments often arose in a common social setting. As has been emphasized, rank-and-file abolitionists were usually cash-crop farmers, artisans, and commercial men—people who embodied occupational versatility, evangelical Protestantism, and rising status. Some of the same generalizations apply to the populations where anti-Southern feelings first developed as burning political concerns. Northern Ohio's Western Reserve and Firelands areas, western and upstate New York's "Burnt-Over District," portions of western Vermont, southern and central New Hampshire, and western Massachusetts became hotbeds of anti-Southern hostility and centers of abolitionist recruitment as the repression continued.

Although settled at widely separate times, each of these regions had been founded by Puritan New Englanders. Usually of nondescript background, these transplanted Yankees had carried with them pronounced preferences for family farming, evangelical religion, and New England institutions. By the 1830's, homogeneous Protestant populations still dominated, but momentous economic developments had overtaken all these locations. Each had developed from a cluster of back-country hamlets and isolated homesteads into mature centers of capitalist agriculture and commercial enterprise. Self-sufficient family farming had given way almost entirely to specialized cash crops. In the band of territory which extended from northeastern Ohio through upstate New York, recently opened canals and a burgeoning lake-shipping trade stimulated regional interdependence. New urban markets were created which ran from Cleveland through Erie, Rochester, and Syracuse to Utica and Albany. By the mid-1820's, vastly improved water and land routes had also tied what were to become the antislavery regions of rural Vermont, New Hampshire, and Massachusetts to urban centers.

Small-town life in these areas also witnessed profound alteration. Oswego, New York; Ashtabula, Ohio; Pittsfield, Massachusetts; and Dover, New Hampshire, are excellent examples of crossroad villages which were transformed into important commercial and manufacturing centers and into beehives of abolitionism. Serving the farmers in the hinterland, newspapers proliferated in all these smaller towns and created sophisticated networks of communication. They also gave literate citizens a heightened sense of involvement in national issues, such as the mobbing of abolitionists and the ransacking of mailbags. Literacy was also widespread. Unusually large concentrations of public schools and private academies furnished children with skills essential to success in this dynamic society.

Viewed from these bustling towns and prospering countryside, the disruptions of the 1830's seemed particularly unwelcome. Understandably, citizens of these regions had come to place a premium on the virtues of individual enterprise and social mobility. Indeed, many of them could claim that by their own honest toil they had risen from obscure beginnings to respectability. Material progress, they firmly believed, depended on the efforts of "free laborers"— self-employed farmers, artisans, and workers. So did the other hallmarks of a "civilized" society—evangelical piety, family stability, republican governance, and the diffusion of secular knowledge. To them, economic advance, the spread of learning, and orderly republicanism were indistinguishable from God's benevolent plans for mankind.

Judged against these values, the ethos of the plantation and the repression of the abolitionists seemed disturbingly related and equally obnoxious. The mobs and censorship efforts quickly came to represent to these Northerners the spirit of slavery itself. Repressive activity encouraged the view that widespread attempts were being made in both the North and the South to exercise a form of arbitrary, unchecked power not unlike that enjoyed by a master over his black chattel. And what did the planter class seem to embody, after all, but the most fundamental denial of "free-labor" ideals? Searching for the first cause of the melees which had suddenly begun erupting in their orderly communities, many Northerners, but especially those in the new, inland commercial centers, fixed upon the planter aristocracy. Perceived as parasites living on the labor of over two million slaves, the planter class seemed to fatten its purses and augment its political strength. Meanwhile, the rest of the whites—impoverished, ignorant victims of this retrograde society—looked listlessly on, mute and helpless. Instead of building stable families and enforcing strict morality, the planters, debauched by idleness, were believed to vent their unbridled lusts in the gaming rooms, at the race tracks, in the taverns, and especially, late at night among the women in the slave quarters. The rewards for the capture of abolitionists, the broken printing presses, the rifled mailbags, and the murdered Lovejoy thus seemed to reflect the unrestrained excesses of the South, as slaveowners began to project their perverted values into the very fabric of Northern society. Gerrit Smith, from the heart of the "Burnt-Over District," articulated his neighbors' misgivings when he announced in 1836 that, in light of recent events, Northerners must now oppose slavery "in self defense." "If it not be overthrown," he warned, the planter class would continue in its "aggression . . . and effectually prepare the way for reducing northern laborers into a herd of slaves."

Abolitionists understood the general characteristics of this emerging antislavery constituency and took steps at once to encourage its progress. They felt increasingly sensitive to what Elizur Wright, Jr., described as the "small men" of the towns and countryside. James G. Birney, for instance, advised a hostile critic in late 1835 that the mobs would fail to silence the abolitionists. "We have only to fly to the *country*," Birney asserted, "to be welcomed by the warm and honest hearts of our yeomanry, and by the artisans and inhabitants of the smaller villages." Accordingly, abolitionists also began to concentrate their campaigns in these centers of rural capitalism. The seventy agents dispatched under Theodore Weld's direction by the American Anti-Slavery Society, for example, focused their efforts between 1835 and 1837 in northern Ohio and upstate New York. The Massachusetts Anti-Slavery Society likewise concentrated on that state's western regions. As these new constituents began to voice concern over slavery, abolitionists also took measures which translated these new, unfocused antislavery feelings into concrete acts of personal involvement. Such acts in turn set off a series of reactions which began to disrupt politics, interjecting antislavery as a new and portentous issue.

The vehicle which abolitionists employed to set off this disruptive process in politics was the legislative petition. Petitions had constituted a vital part of the Northern emancipation movement during the eighteenth century, and memorials encouraging sanctions against slavery had continued into the 1820's. Sensitive to these precedents, the Declaration of Sentiments of the American Anti-Slavery Society had also pledged abolitionists to voice their desire to legislative bodies by affixing their names to petitions. In the earliest years, abolitionists had signed and forwarded to Congress a considerable number of requests for action against slavery in the District of Columbia, the interstate slave trade, the "three-fifths compromise," and the admission of new slave states. By late 1835, the volume of these petitions had grown sufficiently to provoke sectional discussion on the floor of Congress, for in that year the American Anti-Slavery Society had begun to encourage the many newly created state and local societies to carry out campaigns. The next year the number of petition signatures rose to over thirty thousand; sectional debates on the floor of the House of Representatives grew increasingly common and intemperate. By mid-1837 a broad network of local abolition societies, profiling the rising antislavery constituency, extended from northern Ohio along the Erie Canal through western New York and into New Hampshire. In May 1837 the American Anti-Slavery Society announced plans for an intensified national effort, one which relied on local volunteers to circulate the petitions while the staff of the parent society acted as coordinators.

As Gilbert Hobbes Barnes observed many years ago, the importance of local initiative, community involvement, and the individual act of affixing one's signature to an antislavery protest is difficult to overstress. As a result of such activity, large numbers of people became sympathetic to the abolitionists and hostile to the South. Most petitions were carried from door to door by locally known volunteers. The petitions themselves, especially those regarding the ending of slavery in the District of Columbia and the ban on admitting new slave states, were drawn up so that all people suspicious of Southern institutions, not only formally declared immediatists, could sign them. In sectionally conscious neighborhoods, these were subjects upon which, as Elizur Wright, Jr., put it, "all classes, Abolitionists, Colonizationists, Mongrels, and Nothingarians can agree." Women became especially active in circulating petitions, signing them, sending out the forms; in the process, they began to develop a new autonomy and political consciousness. Male abolitionists, unaware of the deeper significance of such activities, encouraged them: "If the ladies . . . really take the business in hand, *it will go*," they believed. Lydia Maria Child, Elizabeth Cady (soon to marry Henry B. Stanton), Lucretia Mott, and a very young Susan B. Anthony took the challenge to heart and successfully tested their leadership and managerial expertise. In smaller towns and farmsteads, thousands of less famous women did likewise. Over half of the petitions bore women's signatures, a fact which suggests the depth of community involvement and the strong link between the petition campaign and the soon-to-emerge crusade for women's rights. Intense local participation, individual acts of sectional expression, dialogues with committed immediatists—these were the experiences of the petition campaign which created a permanent constituency for the abolitionists. As it turned out, so did the manner in which Congress treated the antislavery memorials.

By May 1838, after one year of intensive effort, the American Anti-Slavery Society reported, according to historian Gilbert Hobbes Barnes, that an astonishing 415,000 petitions had been forwarded to Washington. Almost two years earlier, well before it found itself deluged by this enormous tide of remonstrance, the House of Representatives had voted that antislavery petitions could not be made the subject of parliamentary debate. When received they were to be automatically tabled. Passed during the height of antiabolitionist violence and in force until late 1844, this was the famous gag rule which was to play such an influential role in sectionalizing American politics and in politicizing abolitionism.

Complex motives and political dealings lay behind the enactment of the gag rule. Some militant slaveholders agitated for an even stronger measure, hoping that the abolitionists' outrage at such a bill would further solidify the white South. Understandably, slaveowning representatives deeply resented petitions which called their way of life an abomination and which proposed measures detrimental to their interests. Moreover, Southern politicians had long ago concluded that all discussion of slavery, whether in mailed pamphlets or on the floor of Congress, posed a grievous threat to the institution. And of course all politicians, Whig and Democrat alike, knew that arguments over slavery generated sectional hostility, shattered party structures, and threatened the Union.

Given this array of interests and convictions, Martin Van Buren, the original architect of the Democratic Party, managed the passage of a gag rule which satisfied all slaveholders, nearly all Northern Democrats, and most Northern Whigs. In response, abolitionists throughout the North, and especially those in areas of already intense sectional awareness, only redoubled their petitioning efforts and inaugurated the national campaign in 1837. The number of signers jumped dramatically, for the gag rule only added force to abolitionists' warnings that plantation despots connived with "Northern men with Southern principles" to strengthen slavery at the expense of all constitutionally guaranteed liberties. The right of petition, it seemed, along with the rights of free speech, free assembly, and the free press, was collapsing beneath the blows of the "slave power."

The repercussions of the gag rule were quickly apparent. In the House of Representatives, former President John Quincy Adams, now a Whig congressman from Massachusetts, rose to defend the right of petition and freedom of debate. Aged, irascible, and brilliant, "Old Man Eloquent" constantly offered petitions in defiance of the gag rule and thrust the subject of slavery into debate whenever possible. In the Senate, Ohioan Thomas Morris put up a brief and lonely opposition, for which he was efficiently purged from the Jackson party. Adams, by contrast, enjoyed continuous support from constituents and quickly became the recipient of antislavery petitions from all over the North; nearly every other congressman refused to present memorials from their own constituents which violated the gag rule. But in the late 1830's he was joined by several new Whig congressmen, most notably Joshua R. Giddings from Ohio's Western Reserve, Seth Gates from Genesee County in New York's "Burnt-Over District," and William Slade from a heavily "abolitionized" district in Vermont.

The advent of these men in Washington marked a fateful turning point in American politics, one fraught with implications for abolitionists, black and white, for slaveholders and slaves, for politicians of all varieties, indeed for the entire generation that was to witness the coming of the Civil War. The self-propelling cycle of agitation and repression had finally created important pockets of Northern voters who insisted that *their own elected* representatives articulate their stern opposition to slaveholding, to violations of civil rights, and to the political behavior and social values of the planter class. In contradiction to the prevailing intersectional consensus, here were politicians with mandates to debate the morality of slavery, openly and often, regardless of party discipline. Giddings, for example, ran for his first term in Congress on a platform which decried the gag rule, slavery and slave trade in the District of Columbia, and the coastwise slave trade. The Ashtabula County Anti-Slavery Society (organized with the aid of Theodore D. Weld) expressed pleasure at Giddings's "manly and independent stand," and he handily won the first of his nine consecutive terms to Congress.

Self-educated, politically ambitious, and from a poverty-stricken Calvinist family with Connecticut roots, Giddings exemplified the rising social status so commonly found in the broad antislavery movement. His success in law practice and land speculation had neighbors referring to him by the early 1830's as "Squire Giddings." His election marked the demise of the Western Reserve's provincial ex-Federalist elite. As if to reemphasize the point, Giddings chose as his law partner Benjamin Franklin Wade, who also traced his lineage from impoverished Connecticut origins and who had arrived in the Western Reserve as a begrimed member of a canal-digging crew. By 1851 Wade had taken his seat in the United States Senate, a blunt-spoken foe of the planter class.

As the sectional crisis deepened during the 1840's and 1850's, many other politicians with similar backgrounds emerged, relying on the issue of slavery to make their marks in politics. Renegade Democrats like John P. Hale of New Hampshire, Salmon P. Chase of Ohio, Preston King of New York, and David Wilmot of Pennsylvania, as well as dissident Whigs such as Henry Wilson of Massachusetts, George W. Julian of Indiana (later Giddings's son-in-law), Thaddeus Stevens of Pennsylvania, William Seward from New York, and, certainly, Abraham Lincoln could all justly claim to be "self-made men." Belief in the nobility of free labor and economic independence was central to the careers of each and to the lives of the voters who elected them over the next two decades to battle the "slave power." The more the voters supported such politicians, the more difficult it would become for traditional parties to contain sectional ideologies. Giddings demonstrated this fact in 1842 by resigning after receiving congressional censure for his antislavery activities. Rushing home to the Western Reserve, he stood for reelection and was sent back to Washington by a huge majority.

Sectional debates in Congress and the abolitionists' petition campaigns both received great stimulus when in 1835 the independent Texas republic petitioned to be incorporated into the United States. Abolitionists everywhere bridled at including in the American domain this slaveholding territory, which had revolted against Mexican authority. Congressmen like Adams and Giddings also vowed to resist any territorial expansion that would strengthen the plantation economy and augment the slaveholders' political strength. The same tensions which had accompanied the admission of Missouri some fifteen years earlier were reappearing, this time in far more volatile form. The new two-party system depended upon broad voter participation and mass political awareness. As Eric Foner has pointed out, by the 1830's the distance between governors and the governed had narrowed significantly. Thus, even though Whig and Democrat stability did depend on sectional compromise, the dynamics of mass politics also guaranteed that frictions between North and South generated in Washington would rapidly intensify sectional antagonism among the public at large.

Here was a perfect environment in which partisans like John C. Calhoun and John Quincy Adams could exercise maximum influence. As prospects for annexing Texas increased, so did the number of Northerners who voiced adamant opposition. Adams, Giddings, and other Whigs repeatedly warned in widely reprinted speeches that annexation meant more Southern congressmen to vote for the gag rule. Adding Texas also meant creating a new market for slavedealers in the upper South, thus expanding the interstate slave trade and the plantation economy. In sum, Texas annexation simply led to an even greater, more aggressive "slave power." Southern politicians responded that the Constitution had guaranteed full access to the new territory.

Meanwhile, sectionalizing trends also became visible in the abolitionists' petition campaign. Like all their other moral-suasion projects, abolitionists had envisioned this endeavor as a means of changing public attitudes about slavery. In contrast to the postal campaign, however, the thrust of their efforts was now exclusively northward. While most reformers still desired, along with Gerrit Smith, that "the pure and peaceable" principles of abolition would yet "overspread the South," it was clear to them by 1837 that immediatism inspired racial and sectional discord; moral suasion was hardly the soothing balm that they had first imagined. Moreover, it was now clear that, if anything, the white South was more united and the institution of slavery was stronger and better protected than ever before. There was also precious little evidence in support of Garrison's initial prophecy that moral suasion would soon make black skin "popular." The riots and repressions strongly suggested a quite opposite conclusion.

Yet the petition campaign was proving successful in unforeseen ways. Imposing numbers of conventional Northerners were now registering their convictions that slaveowning seriously jeopardized their civil rights, their domestic tranquillity, and their codes of morality. Unlike Wendell Phillips and Edmund Quincy, men "abolitionized" by the mobs, these were not the converts that the abolitionists had initially hoped to create. Not immediatism but a deep hostility toward Southern culture and an abiding suspicion of the planter class defined this new antislavery spirit. Here was a development with enormous potential. Still, it contained ambiguities which all reformers were obliged to ponder. For one thing, these antislavery feelings were as easy to harmonize with race prejudice as with dedication to egalitarian principles. Moreover, people who adopted such views usually stopped far short of radical abolitionism. Though sympathetic to the idea of ending slavery, they often remained suspicious of the "dangerous incendiarism" associated with Garrison, Tappan, Weld, and the rest.

As reformers considered these confusing trends and reflected on the failures of moral suasion, they also began to consider new tactics and formulate new goals. Complicating their deliberations were the attitudes of abolitionist women, who were now insisting on equality within the movement. In addition, there was the problem of violence. What did the repression signify? How as Christians should abolitionists respond to it and to other forms of coercion? In light of their recent experiences, moreover, what should their postures be toward the religious denominations and political parties, all of which had refused to condemn slavery? All these critical problems generated deep ideological conflict, and by mid-1837 factional discords had begun to disrupt the American Anti-Slavery Society. By 1840 the days of abolitionist unity had passed forever.

William Lloyd Garrison, without question, served as the focal point of dissension. It was he who first associated abolitionism with an even more radical opposition to religious and political institutions. As early as 1835, Arthur Tappan had shown discomfort over Garrison's harsh attacks on orthodox New England Calvinists. But by 1837 it seemed to many as if Garrison had begun to act as a magnet of fanaticism, drawing to the cause all manner and mode of eccentricity. Essays which denied the authority of ministers, questioned the authenticity of Scripture, and repudiated the observance of the Sabbath began to appear regularly in the *Liberator*. Garrison's editorials also vigorously endorsed full equality for women. For a time, Garrison considered converting his newspaper into a vehicle for universal reform, not just for abolition, especially since nonresistance, a sweeping denial of all governmental authority, and a religious belief in human perfection also began to command his attention.

With these "exotic" ideas came unconventional people. To be sure, several of Garrison's closest associates—people like Edmund Quincy, Sidney Gay, Ellis Gray Loring and, above all, Wendell Phillips and Maria Weston Chapman—exuded aristocratic refinement. Garrison himself led a rather prosaic life. Yet there was Charles Calistius Burleigh, a close associate of Garrison's, who sported cascading golden curls, a flowing beard, and Old Testament prophet robes. Others of Garrison's circle—rough-hewn New Hampshire farm folk like Parker Pillsbury, Nathaniel P. Rogers, Abby Kelly, and her husband Stephen S. Foster—were extremely disruptive practitioners of moral suasion. Then there were Angelina and Sarah Grimké, Lucretia Mott, and Elizabeth Cady Stanton, and others who defied the woman's "appointed spheres," lectured before audiences of men and women together, and demanded full representation in the antislavery societies. By 1838 it appeared to many in the movement and outside it as if abolitionism, extreme though it was, was about to be overrun by dreamers and cranks.

The reasons for this sudden efflorescence of "isms" beginning around 1837 are several, complex, and not entirely understood. The antiauthoritarian tenor of abolitionism, its general suspicion of venerable institutions, certainly could generate an ever-broadening impulse to question conventional ways. It is certainly instructive to remember that Garrison, in early 1837, found confirmation for his own nonresistance theories in his conversations with John Humphrey Noyes, later the patriarch of the sexually experimental, utopian socialist Oneida Community. The godless authority of masters over slaves and its Christian opposite, black emancipation, thus could become metaphors to express judgments on all human relationships and social institutions. Submission to the worldly discipline of organized governments, political parties, ministers, patriarchical husbands, or one's own private passions seemed no less contrary to God's will than owning a black human being. The goals of self-emancipation and slave emancipation could thus become wholly intertwined, impelling some abolitionists toward espousals of universal reform and, incidentally, toward the vigorous repression of their own sexual drives; abolitionist supporters of women's rights were seldom to confuse their crusade with what some have since come to call a "new morality."

Yet the emergence of iconoclastic radicalism must also be explained in the narrower context of the abolitionists' immediate experiences. The female abolitionists' demand for equality derived as much from their work in the petition campaigns as it did from any general influence of romanticism. In much the same fashion, Garrison and some of his associates contemplated the meaning of antiabolitionist repression and reached disturbing conclusions about American political ideals and religious practices. To these incipient radical abolitionists, violence, gag rules, mail lootings, and denunciations from every religious denomination only revealed the infamy which had overtaken North and South alike. Unlike many immediatists, especially those who were soon to oppose him, Garrison and his supporters put little emphasis on the value of repression in gaining sympathy for the cause. Instead they concluded, as Garrison wrote, that the country deserved "an avalanche of wrath, hurled from the Throne of God, to crush us into annihilation." American Christianity, "mean, dwarfed and corrupt," relied as he put it, on "armed hosts" and engaged in "bloody strife to avenge the slightest threat offered to its *dignity"* by the abolitionists. In Garrison's opinion, Northern Whigs and Democrats, clear barometers of majority opinion, had also reacted much as the mobs and the churches had, "striving to see who will show the most hatred toward us, . . . in order to win southern votes." He now believed that mass opinion, directing the power of church and state, was fostering huge perversions of God's will. Appeals to conscience had to be expanded to induce a total reshaping of the nation's ethical values and institutional practices, a peaceful revolutionizing of every facet of American life. By 1838, Garrison and many other influential immediatists had begun to embrace some of these new positions. Others in the movement shuddered in disgust and began to close ranks against "Garrisonian fanaticism."

The leaders most likely to bridle at "Garrisonism" were the men who had taken primary responsibility in managing the postal and petition campaigns. Lewis Tappan, Joshua Leavitt, James G. Birney, Elizur Wright, Jr., John Greenleaf Whittier, and Henry Brewster Stanton were the most prominent among them. Significantly, but for reasons not entirely clear, Garrison and most of his supporters had not been nearly as deeply involved in these crucial projects even though they had participated actively. Perhaps for this reason Tappan, Birney, and other conservative abolitionists, as they have been called, felt strongly that abolition was progressing in a seriously flawed but basically healthy society. They pointed to the thousands of conventional Northerners, suddenly sensitized to the evils of the "slave power," who were signing petitions, resisting Texas annexation, and supporting the fight against the gag rule. It would be a tactical disaster, they feared, to confuse abolitionism with causes like women's rights and nonresistance. The new antislavery constituency, just taking form, would certainly recoil at such heresies. To conservative abolitionists, moral suasion was coming to mean arousing a mass of reachable Northerners, religious or not. In the meantime, Garrison and like-minded radicals had begun to espouse moral revolution on the totally opposite premise that the people's majoritarian values were themselves the sources of chronic national disease. By 1838, disagreements about strategy and tactics which were far too fundamental for compromise had surfaced in the American Anti-Slavery Society.

Beyond these important questions of strategy, the plain fact was that Garrisonian radicalism repelled the conservatives and threatened them personally. On the question of women's rights, for example, Lewis Tappan and James G. Birney stood fast for masculine dominance and agreed with Elizur Wright, Jr., when he had remarked that the "tom-turkies," not the hens, "ought to do the gobbling." Garrison's rejection of organized religion and the Bible appeared the "rankest infidelity" to evangelical abolitionists like Weld and Tappan. His antigovernment principles and personal refusal to vote seemed invitations to anarchy, in Wright's words, "undermining the whole fabric of social relations." Garrison, for his part, criticized conservative demurrals as evidence of moral atrophy. Inevitably, tensions between reformers and those with radical visions grew more pronounced. By 1838 Stanton, Phelps, Birney, Elizur Wright, Jr., and others wrote freely on how best to purge Garrison and his followers. Garrison, with justice, soon began to complain that "clerical plotters" were conspiring to expel him and his followers.

From early 1838 until the break-up of the American Anti-Slavery Society in May 1840, conspiratorial designs and ideological conflicts overshadowed all else in abolitionism. As Aileen Kraditor has demonstrated, Garrison consistently insisted that abolitionism retain a "broad platform," as he called it. All who pronounced slavery a sin and were dedicated to black equality should be welcomed into the American Anti-Slavery Society, regardless of their opinions on the Sabbath, women's rights, or any other subject. Intent on purging the antigovernment radicals, conservatives insisted to the contrary on a new, restrictive criterion. All true abolitionists, they argued, had a moral duty to vote for candidates sympathetic to the cause. Direct political action should become the focus of abolitionist effort.

By proposing to transform the American Anti-Slavery Society into a political pressure group, conservatives obviously aimed at disqualifying the nonvoting Garrisonians. Yet both the call to political action and Garrison's radicalism were more than weapons employed in factional infighting. So was Garrison's insistence on a "broad platform." By the late 1830's, abolitionism clearly needed new ideas and fresh approaches. With moral suasion in shambles, the continuous rounds of meetings, resolutions, appeals, and remonstrances now seemed soul-deadening and ineffectual. Meanwhile, the petition campaign had become mostly local effort. Garrison's zestful call for a revolutionary reexamination of America's character promised to many abolitionists an imaginative and very necessary new direction.

In the minds of his conservative opponents, the prospect of political activism seemed equally promising, especially since sectional consciousness already seemed so widespread among certain segments in the North. If indirect political pressure of the petition campaign had accomplished this much, conservatives wondered, how much more might be gained by an intensive movement? By 1838 some individuals had even begun talking about a third party based exclusively on abolitionist principles. But whatever its form, any political effort meant attracting antislavery supporters who hardly considered themselves activists. Association with "Garrisonism" would obviously alienate these potential voters.

In July 1840, warring factions of delegates convened in New York City, intent on seizing or breaking up the American Anti-Slavery Society. Both sides packed the meeting, hoping to control the proceedings. Antipolitical Garrisonians, ironically enough, proved the superior political infighters. Radical feminist Abby Kelly was elected to the Executive Committee, 557 to 451, and the defeated conservatives left the society forever. Garrison, far from purged, now presided over a truncated but far more radical body. Most conservatives affiliated with Lewis Tappan's newly formed American and Foreign Anti-Slavery Society, although some, notably Theodore Weld, rejected all factions as self-serving and morally bankrupted.

Meanwhile, Northern concern over Texas annexation, the gag rule, and the menacing "slave power" continued to deepen and spread. The sectional debates in Washington made it clear to both supporters and foes of third-party action that politics and antislavery were rapidly merging. The antislavery constituency was now registering its feelings and would continue to do so on its own or in conjunction with the abolitionists. With some reluctance, conservatives began plans to create a formal political organization, the Liberty Party, to offer authentic abolitionist alternatives in the election of 1840. Garrisonians, in turn, admonished their "apostate" colleagues that slavery and racism could never be overcome at the ballot box without a previous revolution in the moral values of the voters. Antislavery politicians, they warned, would inevitably compromise; winning elections would take precedence over freeing slaves. If, by chance, emancipation was enacted through a political process dominated by the unregenerated, race prejudice would certainly persist, making black freedom a cruel hoax.

As it turned out, sectional conflicts in politics intensified during the 1840's. Liberty Party leaders thus found themselves facing the task of converting antislavery politics into political abolitionism. The extent of their success or failure measured the accuracy of Garrisonian prophecies about politics and black freedom.

5

Abolitionists and the Rise of the Free-Soil Movement

As they entered the election of 1840, leaders of the Liberty Party believed theirs to be an enterprise like no other in American history. They were correct on several grounds. Never before had a party had for its platform the imperative of abolishing slavery. Never had office seekers so completely fused moral absolutes and the vote-getting process. Indeed, one can argue that the Liberty Party exemplified "political antipolitics," a quest for reform no less romantic than the attempt to eliminate slavery and racism with sermons and tracts. Antebellum politics, like most democratic politics, sought common ideological denominators, satisfying to broad and complex constituencies. By contrast, James G. Birney, Gerrit Smith, Joshua Leavitt, Henry B. Stanton, and others in politics urged voters to "come out," to flee the proslavery miasma of Whiggery and Jacksonianism and to cleanse themselves in the atmosphere of political abolitionism.

To Liberty men, the political situation in 1840 surely did seem a clear-cut matter of good and evil. The Democrats had renominated that notorious minion of the "slave power,"

Martin Van Buren, while the Whigs settled on William Henry Harrison, repugnant for his Indian killing as well as for his slaveholding. Contemplating a situation well made for agitation, Liberty men harbored few expectations for their candidate, James G. Birney. Instead, they hoped to attract enough supporters to achieve a balance of power between the two major parties, as they heightened the voters' sensibilities by condemning the sin of slavery.

The Liberty Party platforms are significant because nearly all antislavery politicians eventually upheld them in a moderated form. While endorsing the principle of immediatism, the party nevertheless denied that the federal government had the authority to abolish slavery in the states where it existed. Congress, however, could end slavery and the slave trade in the District of Columbia, terminate the interstate and coastwise slave trades, and bar the admission of new slave states to the Union. This states' rights view, repugnant to all Southerners, was nevertheless the least extreme of several abolitionist theories. A smaller number of political abolitionists always maintained that the congressional power of abolition extended into the slave states proper. From the late 1840's on, some Liberty men also adhered to the rarefied theories of Lysander Spooner, who insisted in his *Unconstitutionality of Slavery* (1845) that all legislation upholding slavery was void since it violated man's natural rights. By contrast, Garrisonian disunionists, who agreed completely with the slaveholders that the Constitution protected slavery in all its aspects, refused to vote and called for a dissolution of the Union.

These Liberty Party and Garrisonian theories, all marred by inconsistencies, reflected again the differences between those who equated abolitionism with reform and those who glimpsed revolution. To condemn the Constitution, as Garrison did, as "A COVENANT WITH DEATH, AN AGREEMENT

WITH HELL," was to demand a new moral order, not to indulge in legal disputation. Liberty men, anxious to support their political reforms, countered by insisting on the Founding Fathers' antislavery intentions. Both groups cited the Constitution much as they quoted the Bible, hoping to induce conversion.

For Liberty men, however, the problem of stimulating repentance quickly became complicated by the obvious fact that most antislavery voters preferred to remain in their accustomed parties. The cause of this reluctance, apparent at once to Liberty men, was that the third party did not speak to other issues of great concern to voters, most importantly those regarding economics. The presence of men such as John Quincy Adams, Joshua Giddings, and Seth M. Gates in the Whig Party indicated that strong opposition to slavery could be made compatible with membership in a national party which addressed these other questions as well. Here was an appeal which the Liberty Party could never hope to equal as long as its platform spoke solely to the issue of slavery. This fact was also obvious to antislavery politicians in the major parties; but their advantage was guaranteed if their own espousals somewhat approximated the intensity of those of the Liberty men.

Reasonably enough, third-party organizers expected to encounter greatest success in precisely those regions where anti-Southern feelings already ran deep. In these districts the Liberty men began offering complete slates of candidates. They also established their own newspapers and began attacking local Whigs and Democrats for their proslavery turpitude. Joshua Leavitt typically warned that the two major parties had already transformed the North into "a conquered province of the slave power," so willing were they to "fawn, spaniel-like before the thrones of the Southern aristocrats." Occasionally, as in the Massachusetts elections during the early 1840's, the third party demonstrated that it could attract enough votes to hold a balance of power. Confronted by such demonstrations, antislavery politicians began to broaden their own sectional espousals, hoping to diminish the Liberty Party's impact. By forcing members of the major parties into increasingly unequivocal positions, Liberty leaders thus began to exercise an influence in politics far in excess of their meager numbers.

Perhaps no politician more aptly illustrates this interplay than Joshua R. Giddings. From 1840 to 1848, Giddings's Western Reserve congressional district had the largest concentration of Liberty Party voters in Ohio; his district also consistently delivered until 1848 the heaviest Whig majorities of any in the state. Yet, early in the 1840's, Liberty men busied themselves in Giddings's stronghold, founding an ably edited newspaper and capturing the support of well-seasoned local politicians like Edward C. Wade, Benjamin F. Wade's strongly antislavery brother, who subsequently stood as Giddings's third-party opponent in several congressional contests. On the state level, Giddings also began to encounter opposition from Gamaliel Bailey, a talented Liberty Party editor whose Cincinnati *Philanthropist* reflected political abolitionist opinion all over the Northwest. From New York City, meanwhile, came the pungent anti-Giddings sentiments of Joshua Leavitt, now editor of the *Emancipator* and a zealous third-party devotee.

From all these sources arose the charge that Giddings's Whig allegiance actually made him a sinful accessory to slavery, not the "friend of freedom" that he claimed to be. Third-party spokesmen cited Giddings's electioneering on behalf of the slaveowning William Henry Harrison, his votes for slaveholders as Speakers of the House of Representatives, and his refusal on constitutional grounds to support repeal of the 1793 Fugitive Slave Law. Voters of Ohio's sixteenth district were thus supporting slavery by casting their ballots for Giddings, Liberty Party spokesmen warned.

To counter these allegations, Giddings began to develop a decidedly sectional line of argument, insisting that his antislavery principles were synonymous with his Whig partisanship. As early as 1840, long editorials appeared over his signature which pictured Whig candidate Harrison as favorable to antislavery measures, such as ending the gag rule and abolishing slavery in the District of Columbia. Democrats like Van Buren were, on the other hand, completely subservient to the South, Giddings maintained, and the Whig Party thus represented the only practical means for political action against slavery. Liberty men only hindered things, he argued, for every vote cast for Birney aided the slave-ridden Democrats by cutting into the Whig electorate.

Similar assertions were made repeatedly as antislavery feelings mounted during the 1840's. In the process, sectional neutrals and Southern politicians became aware of a terrible fact—the third party's antislavery challenge could not be met without allowing explosive sectional ideologies to circulate within existing political structures. Meanwhile, Giddings, Adams, William Slade, and the rest intensified the process by discovering that in comparison to their Liberty Party antagonists, voters perceived them as moderates. Their attitudes toward slavery, certainly radical by all standards of national politics, appeared restrained when compared with Liberty Party extremism. Duly elected agitators thus enjoyed the luxury of speaking as emphatically as they cared to. Suppose he should join the third party, Giddings once challenged a Liberty man, "what advantage could be gained? . . . Could I speak and act more freely, could I be more independent in the declaration of the principles of human rights?" The answer was plainly negative. While Liberty Party organizer's never enjoyed victory at the polls, their local efforts nonetheless gave enormous stimulus to sectionalism within the major parties.

In the early 1840's, however, Leavitt, Stanton, and other political abolitionists began to yearn for satisfying results. Understandably, the 7,059 Liberty Party votes cast in the 1840 presidential election was hardly incentive for redoubled effort. In that election, the only feature of the Liberty Party platform had been the issue of slavery. No matter how wholehearted their abhorrence of slaveholding, voters also maintained passionate opinions on other issues. Especially after 1837, when dislocations began to plague the nation's economy, antislavery voters, like other voters, became anxious to know how candidates stood on such matters as banking, tariffs, and public land policy. A party which remained mute on such important questions was not going to get many supporters.

The Whigs, of course, encouraged voters to fix blame on the Democrats, the party in power when depression first took hold; antislavery Whigs also found a variation of this tactic extremely useful in their struggles with the Liberty Party. The ruinous banking, tariff, and land policies of the Democrats, they maintained, were the result of a party exclusively dedicated to forwarding the perverse interests of "slave labor." Protective tariffs, national banks, federally sponsored internal improvements, and equitable homestead laws, on the other hand, reflected the Whig commitment to the interests of "free labor" and "Northern rights." Their economic programs, such Whigs asserted, were as much antislavery measures as abolishing slavery in the District of Columbia or repealing the gag rule.

Alongside such a broad antislavery statement, the Liberty Party's "one idea" certainly appeared sectarian, especially since the rising antislavery constituencies already possessed such strong preferences for a nationally uniform capitalist economy. Largely for this reason, most antislavery voters during the early 1840's demonstrated an unshakable Whiggishness. To them, Whig economic measures meant overcoming economic parochialism with federal power. The states' rights and laissez faire programs of the Democrats, on the contrary, stirred images of slaveholding "nullifiers" busy in the Southern hinterlands opposing projects designed to forward the legitimate interests of independent farmers, artisans, and professional men everywhere. The same slaveholding interests which were already subverting the civil rights of blacks and Northern whites were now pictured as making war on their economic security through the Democratic Party.

As Liberty men and Garrisonians always contended, the notion that the Whig Party stood for abolition was patently erroneous. Both major parties depended for survival on an intersectional alliance of voters and the slaveholder's goodwill. Yet there was great merit to the antislavery Whigs' contention that using federal power to stimulate free labor was deeply subversive of slaveholders' interests. For one thing, as the Nullification Crisis had demonstrated, many planters now equated the exercise of federal authority over the economy with the possibility of nationally legislated emancipation. Moreover, antislavery politicians were now beginning to develop this Whig economic program as yet another level of conflict between their own expansive society and the hierarchical slave South.

Contemplating these matters, Liberty men proved no less receptive to economic arguments than most other antislavery Northerners. From the first, abolitionists had entertained glowing visions of a nation wholly redeemed and fruitfully improved by universally free labor. Now, in the early 1840's, it was becoming clear to third-party leaders that abolitionism was fast becoming entangled with these broader economic issues. By 1842, Joshua Leavitt, Gamaliel Bailey, and especially Salmon P. Chase of Ohio were complaining openly of the crippling effects of the "one idea" platform. Hoping to attract new supporters, the *Emancipator* and *Philanthropist* began featuring editorials which warned of slavery's exploitative influences upon Northern workers. As early as 1840, Leavitt began admonishing his readers that American economic policy since the election of Jefferson had been "originated by the Slave Power" in order to "make free labor cheap, without lowering the price of cotton." The axiom, endorsed by both major parties, that slave and free labor could prosper "under the same policy" was "just as absurd as perpetual motion, as visionary as the philosopher's stone," he asserted. Soon Liberty Party journals, convention resolutions, speeches, and pamphlets echoed the antislavery Whig appeal: as bloated planter aristocrats fattened their treasuries with the fruits of slave labor, they conspired simultaneously to stifle Northern agriculture, to depress Northern commerce, and to drain off the wages of the Northern working man. Here, Liberty men hoped, were some compelling new arguments which would increase Birney's totals next election day.

A subtle, but unmistakable change was overtaking political abolitionism. Moral agitation on behalf of the slave, the original version of immediate emancipation, was now being moderated in editorials like Leavitt's by a deep suspicion of Southern designs on the welfare of Northern whites. The Garrisonians' original warnings were indeed proving true. Liberty men were discovering that to make an impact at the polls required the compromise of egalitarian doctrines. No revolution in moral values was necessary to oppose the "slave power" on the basis of its threats to "Northern rights"; such opposition, in fact, required little sympathy for the slave in the South and even less for the free black in the North.

To be sure, individual Liberty men such as Birney, Leavitt, John Greenleaf Whittier, Gerrit Smith, William Goodell, and Lewis Tappan continued to act steadfastly on deep commitments to black emancipation and race equality. Liberty Party conventions likewise continued to pass resolutions which condemned discrimination in the North as well as Southern enslavement. As we shall see, even many leading antislavery Whigs and Democrats, while hardly consistent egalitarians, often held to views which also were far in advance of the majority's racist norms. The initial idealism of abolitionism on matters of race was never to be wholly absent from antislavery politics. Yet embedded in this sensitivity to "Northern rights" were also the makings of a white supremacist's antislavery, an ideology in which racism and sectionalism could easily reinforce one another. Leaders of the Liberty Party did generally succeed in maintaining an emphasis on slavery as a terrible violation of human rights. But after 1848 their successors, first in the Free-Soil Party and then the Republican Party, would be far more inclined to view slavery as a menace to white society, while expressing contempt for black-skinned people.

Judged in this context, the Garrisonians' hopelessly utopian emphasis on transforming the racial opinions of the people, not manipulating their voting habits, seems disconcertingly well informed. Still, it also seemed just as impossible to abolitionists as it seems to us today to imagine emancipation except by federal government action of some sort. Practicality dictated that all abolitionists, Liberty men and radicals alike, develop positive responses to the onset of sectional politics. By the early 1840's, abolitionists of all persuasions had begun to discover new and sophisticated political strategies that consciously aimed at influencing the content of anti-Southern feeling as it spread in the two major parties.

Liberty Party leaders quickly hit upon the technique of supporting in private the same antislavery politicians that they opposed so bitterly in public. From the moment that he replaced Birney as editor of the *Philanthropist*, Gamaliel Bailey offered one rebuke after another to these dissident congressmen, denouncing their "proslavery subservience." Meanwhile, he was writing personally to Adams, Slade, Gates, and the others, imploring them to make antislavery speeches in defiance of the gag rule. "Abolitionists will help you," he assured them, "what we all wish is *action now.*" Then, late in 1841, Joshua Leavitt, now Washington reporter for the *Emancipator*, privately encouraged the antislavery Whigs to organize as a formal faction, a "select committee" on antislavery, as Giddings liked to call it. Later, Leavitt would even join this group as it convened in John Quincy Adams's sitting-room. Early in 1842 Theodore D. Weld also joined, serving as a research aide to the antislavery congressmen who, as Leavitt wrote, were now "thoroughly aroused" and ready to agitate a "whole field" of subjects.

Thanks in part to political abolitionists like Leavitt, Whig leaders found themselves incapable of suppressing the party's antislavery wing. Their attempt to censure Adams for presenting antislavery petitions resulted instead in an eleven-day "trial" in which the former President mounted as his defense one rhetorical disquisition after another on the perniciousness of the "slave power." When Adams was "acquitted" on a purely sectional vote, Whigs and Democrats tried to reestablish party discipline by voting to censure the less influential Giddings. Giddings had certainly provided a suitable occasion, for he had offered resolutions affirming the right of slaves to rise in violent mutiny when being shipped in the coastwise slave trade. Resigning his seat, Giddings was overwhelmingly reelected by his Western Reserve constituents. Liberty men, in this instance, dropped their opposition and voted for him en masse.

By 1842 nonvoting Garrisonians had also evolved some surprisingly sophisticated strategies which allowed them to force their romantic radicalism into the arena of sectional politics. In contrast to the Liberty Party, their aim was to influence political action without moderating their own commitments to immediate emancipation and racial equality. To this end, Garrison, Wendell Phillips, and many of their associates in the American Anti-Slavery Society concentrated on arousing the constituencies of antislavery politicians while they mercilessly criticized the politicians themselves, deplored their weaknesses, and jeered at their compromises.

When politicians did serve the abolitionist cause, however, radicals were quick to offer praise and support. For example, when Giddings had been censured and was standing for reelection, Garrison urged that he "be returned by an overwhelming (it ought to be unanimous) vote." Agents of the American Anti-Slavery Society then rushed to his district, hoping to rouse the voters by preaching antigovernment radicalism. Edmund Quincy explained this aspect of Garrisonian tactics well, asserting that the best way to encourage antislavery malcontents in the major parties was to preach radical doctrine to their electorates, aiming thereby to make "their conscience uncomfortable." "In nine out of ten cases," he observed, people thus affected would allay their guilt by casting ballots for antislavery candidates. Acting in this fashion, Garrisonians remained unfettered by political ties and enjoyed the widest possible freedom to influence sectional politicians in all parties. Even as racism became increasingly compatible with political antislavery, Garrisonians remained successful in thrusting before the voters the uncompromised ideal of black emancipation.

The radicals' political tactics served other important ends. By demanding "No Union with Slaveholders," Garrisonians lessened a polemical advantage enjoyed by states' rights Southerners. In nearly all circles outside radical abolitionism, Northern responses to the slaveholders' secession threats had always smacked of musty legalism, as congressmen solemnly affirmed the perpetuity of Union. Garrisonians hoped to correct this imbalance in the sectional debate by reminding Northern politicians that constitutional literalism was no substitute for confronting slavery. As Quincy put it tersely in 1847, "Calhoun in the South and Garrison in the North stand front to front . . . Every man must needs be on one side or the other." Northerners who sought a middle ground in sectional debates found their positions assailed, not just by slaveholding extremists, but by radical Garrisonians as well.

Southern politicians, after all, sat high in national councils and threatened secession to protect slavery. In opposing such threats while abstaining from voting, Garrisonian agitators aimed to make antislavery politicians and the voters aware that they, too, must appeal from constitutional writ to some God-given "higher law." Here, then, was serious political activity, wholly compatible with the romantic individualism which Garrisonians so faithfully personified.

Whatever their ideological differences, all abolitionists and most politicians agreed that slavery questions bore heavily upon the 1844 presidential election. Since 1840, antislavery feeling had been stimulated by the gag-rule struggles, by several spectacular slave mutinies on the high seas, and by increased reluctance in the North to enforce the 1793 Fugitive Slave Law. In 1842 the Supreme Court ruled in *Prigg vs. Pennsylvania* that the power to legislate the return of fugitives lay exclusively with Congress. New Hampshire, Connecticut, Rhode Island, Pennsylvania, Vermont, and Massachusetts consequently enacted "personal liberty laws," denying federal authorities any state assistance when recapturing slaves. Of little practical value to the escapees, these laws nonetheless testified to the increasing resentment of Northerners toward slaveowning politicians. In this setting, it is hardly surprising that large numbers of voters bridled at the renewed prospect of adding another slave state, Texas, to what seemed an already formidable "slave power."

The fate of Henry Clay, the Whig nominee for President, is a good example of how sectionalism began taking its toll in national politics. By instinct a traditional party leader, Clay sought to suppress antagonisms between his Northern and Southern supporters. With his probable Democratic opponent, Martin Van Buren, Clay took steps to remove the issue of the annexation of Texas from the election; both men issued ambiguous statements, hoping to end discussion on the question. The Democrats, however, surprised Clay by casting Van Buren aside and nominating instead the Tennessee slaveholder James K. Polk on an expansionist platform which called for the immediate annexation of Texas. Hoping also to satisfy the North, the party pledged to acquire all of Oregon as well, a region claimed by England which was clearly not hospitable to plantation settlement.

By endorsing these acquisitions, the Democrats were responding to some of the dominant impulses of the 1840's. Ever since 1819, when the Florida territory had been annexed, the boundaries of the United States had remained fixed. But by the mid-1840's, a new spirit of aggressive nationalism proclaimed that America's "manifest destiny" lay in occupying the entire continent. Many contradictory motives lay behind this thrust for continental dominion. Historians cite the land-hunger of pioneers, Eastern desires for Pacific commercial bases, and fears of European encroachment on the West Coast. To many slaveholders, moreover, expansion offered the promise of replacing acreage in the older slave states which was being exhausted by overcultivation. To create new slave states out of Western territories would also enhance the South's political dominance in the Union. While oppposed to these goals, many Northerners nevertheless endorsed expansion as the best way to promote the well-being of free laborers and republican institutions. Western territories should be distributed at low cost to individual settlers to alleviate problems of urban poverty and to prevent artificial concentrations of wealth.

In promising to annex Texas and occupy Oregon, the Democrats thus attempted to accommodate the conflicting ideals of the slave plantation and the family farm, a dangerous experiment indeed. Instead of mollifying sectional passions, their aim was now to manipulate them for partisan advantage over Henry Clay. This platform, as all informed citizens knew, also increased the likelihood of war with Mexico, for that nation still refused to recognize the independence of its former province. American military success, in turn, could bring even greater territorial acquisitions. So could any war of conquest with England which might develop over the disposition of Oregon. Some even spoke excitedly of annexing British-held Canada and carving it into free states.

In the midst of these developments, a better-organized Liberty Party renominated Birney on a broadly anti-Southern platform which emphasized the "slave power's" sinister role in promoting the annexation of Texas. Clay now had to worry about defections in the North as well as in the South as his supporters pressed him to make clear his own position on sectional issues. To the discomfort of slaveholders everywhere, Northern spokesmen of both parties emphasized their own anti-Southern positions, hoping thereby to minimize the Liberty Party vote. Antislavery Whigs issued extravagant claims for Clay as an antislavery man, even picturing him as anxious to abolish slavery in the District of Columbia.

Embarrassed by his own supporters, Clay could only hedge and shift, hoping to keep his coalition together. Significant numbers of Whig voters responded with increasing disgust at Clay's "slippery tactics." "He is as rotten as a stagnant fishpond on the subject of slavery and always has been," Seth M. Gates declared as he renounced his Whig allegiance and voted for Birney. And it was voters precisely like Gates who doomed Clay's campaign. Enough of them in New York switched from Clay to Birney to give that state's thirty-six electoral votes, and the presidency, to James K. Polk.

Liberty Party abolitionists like Lewis Tappan claimed at the time that they preferred as President "an out and out friend and advocate of slavery" like Polk to "an intriguer" like Clay. Yet the significance of this election lay far less in who got the most votes than in how the political process had begun to work. Ideologues in substantial numbers had begun to make pro- and anti-slavery demands within both major parties. For a decade longer, orthodox political loyalty would prove strong enough to withstand the corrosive passions of sectionalism. Yet in the defeat of Henry Clay in 1844 lay clear portents of elections to come.

By mid-1846 Texas had been annexed, Polk had opened military hostilities against Mexico, and opposition to the "slave power's" further expansion had begun to deepen throughout the North. Abolitionists of all sorts, New England's intelligentsia and hard-bitten Whigs and Democrats, agreed that behind Polk's administration stood a united planter class directing warfare aimed only at furthering Southern interests. Theodore Parker and James Russell Lowell wrote cleverly and spoke eloquently, denouncing Polk's actions against Mexico, while Henry David Thoreau, who deemed the war an affront to his pacifism, spent a night in jail rather than support the government by paying his poll tax. Garrisonians, of course, took satisfaction in trumpeting that the war only proved once again what they had known all along—that all political parties and governmental instruments, like all American institutions, were hopelessly corrupted by slaveowning. It remained as impractical as ever, so Garrison wrote, to expect "tyrants and the enemies of tyranny to coalesce and legislate for the preservation of human rights. . . . The motto enscribed on the banner of Freedom should be NO UNION WITH SLAVEHOLDERS!"

Few Americans ever followed Garrison's advice literally. Yet as events of the Mexican War years built toward a sectional confrontation, more and more Northerners came to similar conclusions. While disavowing radical abolitionism, antislavery Yankees began to feel increasingly compelled by their own "higher" allegiances to "Northern rights" to sever their associations with proslavery organizations. Loyal Whigs and Democrats soon experienced further fragmentation as their antislavery wings threatened secession. Politicians and reformers not given to Garrisonian forms of radicalism also came to express disturbing views about the nature of the Union.

In 1846, Wendell Phillips noted these trends approvingly, writing that Northerners who once "would have whispered Disunion with white lips now love to talk about it." Many "leading men," he predicted, "will soon talk as we were once laughed at for talking. . . ." Phillips, in fact, was understating matters. Even before the 1844 elections, twelve Northern congressmen, led by Adams, Gates, and Giddings, had issued a public warning that if Texas were annexed as a slave state, the Union would cease to have a moral basis for existence. With the federal government thus transformed into a "slaveholding despotism," patriotic Americans would have every moral reason to sever their relationships with it. In 1845 the Massachusetts and Ohio legislatures threatened to refuse compliance with the federal statutes which enabled Texas statehood. In 1846 Giddings himself, moreover, treated all politicians to the bewildering spectacle of running successfully for reelection while denying the moral authority of the same government in which he sought to retain his place.

To be sure, Garrisonian disunion was inextricably connected with immediate emancipation, while these "disunionist politicians" objected primarily to adding new slave states. Yet William Jay, a most conservative abolitionist, sensed correctly that all these espousals of disunion reflected a common "state of mind." As Southern demands intensified, greater numbers of Northerners became, like the Garrisonians, willing to question the nation's fundamental assumptions. Could a truly republican government be equally dedicated to the contradictory interests of aristocratic slaveholders and self-sufficient free laborers? Must federal power involve Northern citizens in retrieving the planters' slaves? Must Northern voters be called on, time and again, to endorse and then underwrite programs which promoted the expansion of slavery? Or should "freedom-loving Northerners" rethink the meaning of Union and throw off their shackles of loyalty to a system dominated by the "slave power"?

In religion as well as in politics, the frequency of "coming out," that is, of separating from proslavery institutions, was an excellent measure of personal alienation and sectional pressures. Stephen S. Foster and Parker Pillsbury practiced the doctrine in garish forms of which most other Garrisonians disapproved during the 1840's, by nonviolently disrupting church services in New England with uninvited lectures on slavery. Not uncommonly, members of congregations would first flinch with surprise, then exclaim in outrage as Foster suddenly rose to denounce the clerical establishment in harsh New Hampshire accents. "Thieves, blind guides, and reprobates," he called them, "a cage of unclean birds." Often the parishioners would escort him bodily to the door. More often, abolitionists like Gerrit Smith and Lewis Tappan withdrew from their denominations to found independent "free" churches in which slavery was recognized as a sin. In this fashion Presbyterians, Baptists, and Congregationalists all experienced serious defections in the East and Northwest, and among the Methodists a formal division took place. By 1845 the denomination had split into pro- and anti-slavery wings, largely owing to the agitation of evangelical abolitionists like Orange Scott, Luther Lee, and La Roy Sunderland.

Repelled by clergy's stubborn resistance to immediatism, and the hollow sacramentalism of conventional worship, still other abolitionists sought spontaneous, intensely personal religious experiences—a "coming out" which led to no denominational upheavals. Abolitionists like Theodore D. Weld, Angelina G. Weld, Lydia Maria Child, Elizur Wright, Jr., and many others thus moved toward a diffuse, disorganized "religion of humanity," hoping, as one explained, to be "less orthodox but more Christian" by scrapping formal theology for a pure humanitarian creed. For some seekers the quest led further to espousals of religious anarchism and efforts to build holy communities wherein no discordant human enactments could interrupt the harmony of Divine Law. Abolitionism, religious anarchism, and utopian socialism thus united in the careers of Adin Ballou, John A. Collins, and others. At the same time, as Lewis Perry has shown with such clarity, these yearnings also could radiate through the many circles of abolitionism, third-party men and nonresistants alike. Viewed through this lens of Christian utopianism, all human agencies could seem fatally retrograde, and the power of institutionalized churches was weakened accordingly.

But it was antislavery Northerners in the two major parties, not anticlerical abolitionists, who stirred the most immediate controversies during Mexican War years. Among the Whigs, old insurgents like John Quincy Adams now found support from some aggressive and much younger men. Another Adams, Charles Francis, was prominent among them, and "Old Man Eloquent" was uncomfortably aware that his son wore a Whig allegiance lightly. Ever since 1845, established antisectional Whig leaders from Massachusetts, men like Robert Winthrop, Daniel Webster, and Abbott Lawrence, had found themselves confronted by noisy antislavery opponents, "Conscience Whigs" as they called themselves. Among the latter were men soon destined for careers as the North's foremost sectional politicians—Charles Sumner, Henry Wilson, John G. Palfrey, and the younger Adams. By 1847 these individuals were deep in correspondence with outstate Whig dissidents and also with significant antislavery elements which had begun to form among the Northern Democrats. Both groups in turn began discussing stratagems with Gamaliel Bailey, Joshua Leavitt, Salmon P. Chase, and other Liberty Party leaders.

Among the Northern Democrats, hostility toward their own party's policy of expanding slavery was reinforced by deep political resentment against James K. Polk. Especially in New York, associates of Martin Van Buren, such as Preston King, Silas Wright, and John A. King began voicing concern that their party was rapidly being overrun by the "slave power's" influence. The party's future in the North (and theirs) depended on maintaining the traditional policy of generally supporting slavery while suppressing sectional discord, Van Burenites felt. But from the start, Polk's policies seemed to run in the opposite direction.

As American armies occupied vast stretches of Mexico, Democratic followers of Van Buren in Ohio, Massachusetts, and Pennsylvania also became ever more concerned that their party was becoming unacceptable to Northern voters. Already New Hampshire's Democratic machine was splintering as John Parker Hale, the junior United States senator, flouted party policy by opposing the Mexican War. Polk's unwillingness to satisfy the Van Buren Democrats' patronage expectations, his vetoes of bills to subsidize river and harbor improvements, and his failure to annex all of Oregon seemed in retrospect further signs of the "slave power's" increasing domination of the party.

Most ominous of all, however, was the growth of these feelings in the Van Burenites' constituencies as Whig and Liberty Party opponents began to lure away voters with antislavery appeals. Hoping to arrest the "slave power's" momentum, a group of Northern Democratic representatives introduced in August 1846 the instantly famous "Wilmot Proviso." Named after Pennsylvania Congressman David Wilmot, the Proviso, which never was to pass both houses of Congress before the Civil War, stipulated that slavery be excluded from all territory acquired through war with Mexico.

The demand for "free soil," or territory in which slavery was prohibited, reflected the belief that America's frontier must be preserved for Northern free labor. The Wilmot Proviso served to thrust this issue into the center of American politics. From then on, all agreed that the nation's future depended on whether slaveholding planters or "republican free laborers" shaped the development of this vast region. Opposition to slavery, as Eric Foner has emphasized, was now "coming to focus on its lowest common denominators"—free soil, opposition to the "slave power," and a firm resolve to ensure Northern supremacy within the Union. Here was an ideology capable of uniting otherwise antagonistic interests into a common anti-Southern front; here also was an ideology in which the abolitionist commitment to black equality could have little, if any, formal place.

Liberty men, well aware of these facts, grew increasingly divided and confused as the 1848 presidential election neared. Veterans like James G. Birney, Joshua Leavitt, and Gerrit Smith recalled with disgust Martin Van Buren's sponsorship of the gag rule and his strident antiabolitionism during the 1830's. The unabashed willingness of Van Burenites to support vast territorial conquests from unoffending Mexico in the name of free soil also filled them with misgivings. So did clarifying statements like the one David Wilmot offered in 1846: "I would preserve for free white labor a fair country, a rich inheritance, where the sons of toil, of my own race and color, can live without the disgrace which association with negro slavery brings upon free labor."

Other members of the party, led by Gamaliel Bailey, Henry B. Stanton, and Salmon P. Chase, stressed political "realism" and urged coalition with antislavery Whigs and Democrats. Birney, they advised, though already renominated, should step aside in favor of John P. Hale, a national figure whose Democratic background might just appeal to Van Burenites. Whigs like Charles Francis Adams meanwhile pressed hard for the antislavery Democrats and Liberty men to unite behind any number of "Northern rights" candidates. As Garrisonians kept up a drumfire of reminders that support of free soil meant capitulation to "white man's antislavery," political abolitionists everywhere faced an agonizing decision as to where "realism" lay. Was it found in compromising, by joining and then trying to improve the racist tone of the largest antislavery groundswell to date? If so, then the Garrisonians had a point; pitfalls of expedience lay ahead. Or did "realism" mean maintaining principle, adhering to the doctrines of immediate emancipation and black equality? If so, then the Liberty Party most certainly would appear again, as it had to so many in 1840, as a cranky sect, removed from even the periphery of significant political activity.

In August 1848, Liberty Party abolitionists finally had to choose. By then, the Whig and Democratic leaders, again trying to suppress sectional tensions, had ratified their platforms and selected their candidates. The results, however, guaranteed the defection of the Van Buren Democrats and the antislavery Whigs. Lewis Cass of Michigan, the corpulent old 1812 war hero, received the Democratic nomination on a platform of "popular sovereignty." Seen as a means to remove the slavery issue from national politics, "popular sovereignty" meant transferring from Congress to the people of each territory the responsibility of deciding whether to adopt slavery. Theoretically at least, this doctrine opened to slavery all lands ceded by Mexico in the formal agreement which ended hostilities. The Whigs, by contrast, decided that the best approach to slavery questions was silence; they adopted no platform at all and nominated a politically inexperienced slaveholding general, Zachary Taylor. Voters in antislavery districts clamored for third-party revolt and were ready, as one local correspondent put it, to "pronounce a valedictory on the dead and rotten carcass[es]" of the two national parties. Van Buren Democrats, Conscience Whigs, and Liberty Party leaders thereupon held a presidential convention of their own in Buffalo.

The Free-Soil Party, as the new party called itself, conjoined such diverse political types as Frederick Douglass, Joshua Leavitt, and Martin Van Buren. Here was clear evidence of the Wilmot Proviso's effectiveness in generating antislavery consensus. After much political dealing, the abolitionists' old antagonist, Martin Van Buren, accepted the Free-Soil Party nomination. To satisfy antislavery Whigs like John G. Palfrey and Charles Sumner, the convention chose Charles Francis Adams as Van Buren's running mate. The platform, a far more limited form of antislavery than any the Liberty Party had ever presented, endorsed the Proviso with the slogan "Free Soil, Free Speech, Free Labor, Free Men" and declared that the federal government must "relieve itself of all [constitutional] responsibility for the existence and continuance of slavery." The rest of the platform dealt with those broad economic issues which were now becoming intertwined with antislavery—homestead laws, tariffs, and federally sponsored internal improvements. Still, Liberty men could not help noticing the omission of any pledge to assist free blacks or to work for immediate emancipation. Their time of decision was at hand: whether to join these dissident Whigs and Democrats or to depart from the convention, doctrines intact.

Most chose to stay. Joshua Leavitt in a moving speech urged Liberty Party delegates to believe that their party was simply being "translated" into something larger and more effective without serious loss of principle. Henry B. Stanton, John Greenleaf Whittier, Gamaliel Bailey, and many other political abolitionists with impeccable credentials agreed, campaigned for Van Buren, and imparted to the Free-Soil cause a higher moral tone than it might otherwise have had. Others like Gerrit Smith, William Goodell, and F. Julius LeMoyne could not accept the Free-Soil Party's limited doctrines, its "tainted" candidates, or the expedience on which it had been formed. Leaving the proceedings in protest, they endorsed legislated emancipation and organized themselves as the Liberty League. Their fourth party functioned until 1861 much as the nonvoting Garrisonians did, prodding antislavery politicians and insisting on a redeemed America, free of racism and slavery.

Were men like Leavitt and Bailey misguided in their willingness to compromise their principles with Free-Soil racists? Or was their course a reasonable one, especially when one considers what the character of the party might have been without them? Further, were Smith and the Liberty Leaguers impractical in their decision to "come out" from direct involvement in the mainstream of antislavery? Or was theirs a refreshing example of rectitude in a world too often governed by racism and expedience? Historians who emphatically answer "yes" or "no" to these trying questions usually reveal more about their own opinions on contemporary black-white relations than they do about abolitionism. It is vital to remember the wise observation of Aileen Kraditor that abolitionism's left wing, its Garrisons and Gerrit Smiths, challenged the limits of racial consensus of *their* time, not ours. The same applies to moderates like Leavitt who associated with some of the dominant prejudices of his age while hoping to diminish their effect. By remembering that the abolitionists' world was not ours, we may better understand the nature of our own enormous racial tragedy.

But whatever their attitude toward politics and reform, abolitionists agreed that partisanship was allowed freest reign in the 1848 elections. To a much greater extent than in 1844, Northern spokesmen in the two major parties outdid one another's antislavery professions, seeking to minimize losses to the Free-Soilers. Southern Whigs and Democrats again worried that abolitionism was overtaking their parties. Supporters of the third party in turn mounted a vigorous campaign, aided by the strong regional organizations commanded by such defectors as Giddings in Ohio, Preston King in New York, and John P. Hale in New Hampshire. As in 1844, third-party voting patterns in New York decided the presidential outcome, this time in favor of the Whigs' Zachary Taylor. Although it captured no electoral votes, the Free-Soil Party did win in twelve congressional races. Where its nominees were defeated, it was often by major party candidates like Pennsylvania's Thaddeus Stevens, a Whig who held unshakable antislavery convictions.

This newly elected Congress, so highly charged with North-South antagonism, was the body which had to decide what to do with the lands taken from Mexico. Many slaveholders, alarmed by the continuing progress of emancipation in South America, expressed increasing concern that the South was being encircled by free territory. The South needed to expand westward, they argued, to secure new territory against the forces of worldwide abolitionism. Slaveholders also expected to employ slave labor in the mines of New Mexico and California and in plantation agriculture in the Colorado, Rio Grande, and Gila river valleys. Besides, soil exhaustion and surplus slaves, the political realities of sectional balance, and the promise of huge profits had already driven the slaveholding states to double their area since 1800. As abolitionists watched from the sidelines, bipartisan politicians in Congress struggled to reconcile the contradictory demands of sectional interest and national unity.

The result again was compromise, arranged by conservative politicians who again separated the question of slavery's morality from the political process. Abolitionists everywhere joined in a rising chorus of disgust as Daniel Webster, Henry Clay, and especially Stephen A. Douglas of Illinois passed through Congress a series of measures designed to preserve the political balance between the sections and to bury disputes over slavery forever. "What a travesty on the mathematics of justice," Garrison exclaimed, "to announce excitedly that two and two make six, to argue a bit about it, and then to shake hands on the number five!" Congress voted to admit California to the Union as a free state, while slaveholding Texas, already a state, received ten million dollars for giving up her extensive territorial claims in New Mexico. In New Mexico and Utah, created as new territories, the slavery question was to be solved later by popular sovereignty. As a concession to the North, slavetrading (but not the practice of holding slaves) was prohibited in the District of Columbia. To right the balance, Congress amended the 1793 Fugitive Slave Law to include new, far harsher provisions. The law authorized federal commissioners, not state judges, to process fugitive cases, and every Northern citizen was obliged to assist in the recapture of escapees. Whites who abetted escaped slaves now risked severe penalty, and the fugitives themselves were deprived of the right to trial by jury or opportunity to testify. Free blacks found themselves in clear jeopardy of being summarily claimed as escaped slaves, seized, and shipped South.

Slaveowners correctly saw in this law a sweeping assertion of their power within the Union. The abolitionists agreed entirely with this view. So flagrant was this law's violation of judicial procedure that many Northerners otherwise not hostile to slavery joined in opposing it. As had the gag rule and the antiabolitionist violence of the 1830's and 1840's, the Fugitive Slave Law in the 1850's served to fuse antislavery feeling with a pervasive fear of the "slave power's" dominion in American political life. But most of all, the Fugitive Slave Law reminded apathetic whites through the resistance it provoked that militant black men and women were struggling in both sections to secure freedom and justice for their race. Henry Clay was fond of repeating, in the aftermath of the Compromise of 1850, that permanent peace now prevailed "throughout all of our borders." At the same time, black abolitionists, white sympathizers, and the slaves themselves began committing acts which destroyed Clay's vision of permanent domestic tranquility.

6

Race, Class, and Freedom in American Abolitionism

In October 1851, Jerry McHenry, a free black resident of Syracuse, New York, was seized by federal marshals acting under the Fugitive Slave Law. Six hours later he found himself on the road to Canada, liberated by a crowd of indignant blacks and whites which had successfully stormed his jail cell. Gerrit Smith and Samuel J. May had contrived Jerry McHenry's rescue with black abolitionists Samuel Ringgold Ward and Jermain Loguen. Subsequently, twenty-six individuals were indicted for violating the law—twelve black, fourteen white.

Incidents even more dramatic than the Jerry McHenry rescue in Syracuse were to punctuate the 1850's, promoting militant black-white collaboration against the "slave power." Yet, long before this decade of violence, abolitionists of both races had fully tested the limits of interracial harmony. Cooperation, black and white reformers discovered, was often natural and inevitable. In certain instances it could be immensely beneficial. But as often as not, blacks and whites found themselves working at cross-purposes, divided by some of the racial antagonisms and class tensions that circulated in antebellum America.

In their excellent study of antebellum black activism, Jane and William Pease have emphasized the existence of "two abolitionisms": one white, one black. White abolitionists sensed a total antithesis between the concepts of slavery and freedom; the one was evil incarnate, the other partook only of God's perfect grace. Moreover, enslavement and emancipation paralleled other pairs of moral opposites— guilt and innocence, damnation and salvation, sublimation and self-liberation. This value system, based on fixed abstractions, made it difficult for whites to fathom what so many black activists understood by the term "freedom."

Drawing on lifetimes of discrimination, blacks were painfully aware that complete freedom and formal enslavement represented extremes of condition. Between them, the Peases write, "lay a vast and variegated spectrum, . . . more or less freedom and more or less slavery." The difficult requirements of survival simply left no reason to dwell upon abstract categories. White abolitionists, never having felt caste oppression, found it difficult to understand that through exclusion from juries, elections, decent schools, and gainful employment, Northern blacks continuously experienced enslavement by racism. For blacks far more than for whites, bondage in the South and discrimination in the North were two aspects of the single national problem of racism. Their day-to-day actions in the North therefore took on a pragmatism which no white reformers could ever wholly fathom.

The white reformers' cultural ethos and successful class position often added to racial separation. The sincere egalitarian professions of men like Wendell Phillips, the Tappan brothers, and William Lloyd Garrison must always be placed in the context of a Northern white Protestantism unable to conceptualize what in a later age would be called "cultural pluralism." As we have seen, white abolitionists always placed a premium on achieving a morally homogeneous society. Provincial cultures as well as pockets of ethnicity and poverty—the poor Southern whites, the English urban poor, and the Irish immigrants to America, for example—provoked impulses to preach of "a better way." Given their generally secure social position, enormous bureaucratic skills, and belief in the power of conversion, it would be surprising indeed if even the most sympathetic white abolitionists had not attempted to make over the lives of black Americans. It was natural for them to assume that black culture had little to recommend it and that blacks needed benevolent guidance in working hard, feeling pious, and avoiding vice.

Most Northern black leaders chose a degree of accommodation with the whites' stern moral designs. Whites looked on approvingly as black activists worked tirelessly throughout the North, organizing Bible societies and other benevolent associations which replicated white organizations. Yet compliance was a complex matter, often misleading to whites and hardly tantamount to "selling out the race." Indeed, in the process of accommodation could be found the seeds of further estrangement. White responses to black efforts in temperance reform provide a clear illustration of the point.

In temperance, black leaders found a national cause, also popular with white reformers, which held personal meaning and community promise. By the 1840's, blacks had created statewide temperance societies in Connecticut and New York, as well as an additional organization which embraced these two states and Massachusetts. Every major Northern city contained similar organizations, and so did many smaller towns. In Cincinnati, fully one-quarter of the black population had "taken the pledge," avowing that in abstinence from alcohol lay the surest path to honesty, modesty, thrift, and Christian rectitude.

Lewis Tappan or Gerrit Smith could not have felt more warmly benevolent toward "noble sentiments" such as these. Yet these black espousals of Protestant values reflected no desire necessarily to curry favor with pious philanthropists and certainly no belief that drunkenness was a burden peculiar to black society. Instead, black leaders in temperance often acted out of race pride, challenging the black community to gather its resources, to demonstrate its vitality, and to channel its capital from personal consumption to income-producing enterprise. Too often, white abolitionists did mistakenly see in these activities only cheering evidence that "moral uplift" was proceeding apace, and their own paternalism, thereby reinforced, only became more burdensome to their black associates. As former slave Henry Highland Garnet once exploded at a patronizing white abolitionist who criticized his espousals of armed resistance and black self-assertion in politics:"It astonish[es] me to think that you should desire to sink me again to the condition of a *slave* by forcing me to think as you do."

But, as Garnet and other black abolitionists knew, behind the insults of paternalism often lay more destructive forms of racism. In the antebellum years, most Caucasians embraced racist doctrines with considerable intensity. When white abolitionists committed themselves to oppose all prejudice, it is certainly not surprising that they proved unable to discern the extent of their own biases. Instead, even in the language of most enlightened white abolitionists like Wendell Phillips, echoes of unconscious white superiority could be detected.

Phillips's aristocratic temperament led him to belittle practically anybody from Daniel Webster on down. On this ground, his derision of a black associate's clothing must be dismissed; he did the same to some of his white colleagues. Moreover, his devotion to Garrisonian strategies, not racism, was what led him once to slander J. W. C. Pennington, a black Liberty Party organizer; he always assumed the worst about Liberty Party leaders. In short, Phillips displayed no conspicuously antiblack sentiments. Yet in his speeches, so compelling in content, so beautifully delivered, so enormously popular, lay themes which emphasized the almost mystical Anglo-Germanic nature of America's heroic history and destiny, which celebrated the Teutonic-Puritan sources of American democracy. In 1859, for example, Phillips called for bold action against the South and spoke for the exercise of "an element in Yankee blood, an impulsive, enthusiastic aspiration, something left to us from the old Puritan stock." It was this essence, he believed, "which made England what she was two centuries ago" and which would sustain the North in "the closest grapple with the Slave Power today." Redemption of the South would "come from the interference of [this] wiser, higher, more advanced civilization" which had first "crept around our shores" from England in the 1600's.

Here, then, was a cultural attitude clearly short of racism, but which those who heard Phillips could nonetheless put to destructive purposes. Theodore Parker, for example, developed most of his militant abolitionism on the assumption that emancipation of the inferior black race would usher in a glorious new era of Anglo-Saxon dominance. As George Fredrickson has shown, this "romantic" racism was often appropriated by all classes and regions, circulating widely within white abolitionism as well. Hence, as they tried to manage antislavery societies, found newspapers, and develop projects of agitation, black and white abolitionists constantly found themselves driven apart by the forces of race and class.

Initial appreciation of the white immediatists for attacking colonization soon diminished among black abolitionists as they began to notice how underrepresented they were in the antislavery societies. Discomfort heightened in the later 1830's as conservatives involved themselves in white civil liberties issues while radicals expounded women's rights and perfectionism. Both groups, distracted, now did less about the Northern racial situation. The *Colored American*, edited by Samuel D. Cornish, hotly asserted that these new questions were *"neither parts nor parcels"* of the struggle for black freedom. In 1843, Frederick Douglass and another talented black orator, Charles L. Remond, clashed openly with white Garrisonian John A. Collins, denying Collins's contention that his espousals of Christian socialism should supersede discussions of black emancipation at antislavery gatherings. Nor was this debate purely ideological. The Boston bluestocking Maria Weston Chapman, along with other white Garrisonians, paternalistically "forgave" Douglass and Remond their anger, dismissing their dissent as reflecting a lack of intellectual sophistication and disadvantaged backgrounds.

It is easy to cite other incidents which illustrate the limits of the white immediatists' commitments to racial equality. Garrison's denunciations of Frederick Douglass for endorsing the Liberty Party is only one of the most well known. Insisting that there was "a roguery somewhere," Garrison denounced Douglass's independent decisions as "destitute of every principle of honor, ungrateful to the last degree, and malevolent in spirit." Another oft-cited instance of white abolitionist racism is Arthur Tappan's consistent failure to hire blacks for responsible positions in his mercantile enterprise.

Yet if much is made of these examples of the abolitionists' own discriminatory acts on the grounds of their hypocrisy, another extremely important fact should not be forgotten. Genuine interracial understanding has been rare in the United States, accomplished by only the most discerning of both races. One can never know whether discomfort or respectful understanding was more often the result of Weld's or Garrison's habit when traveling of boarding in the homes of black abolitionists. One can likewise only imagine what black and white undergraduates at Oberlin discovered about themselves and one another during their years in college. What is certain is that it gains little to blame the abolitionists because of their prejudices for America's continuing race problems. Hampered in their time by culture, class, and pigmentation, many abolitionists of both races nevertheless explored the furthest boundaries of egalitarianism allowed by their age. That their efforts often led to frustration, not biracial utopia, should hardly surprise us.

Most often, black abolitionists put their frustrations with white colleagues to constructive purpose. By the 1830's they had established institutions and programs in which they, not the whites, determined policy and which served the ends of freedom as the black community understood them. Some of the earliest manifestations of this trend appeared in the National Negro Convention Movement, launched in 1830 and destined to experience periods of relapse and resurgence into the twentieth century. The antebellum history of this enterprise gives some insight into the evolving nature of black abolitionism.

The first National Conventions, which gathered from 1830 to 1835, were dominated by wealthy free blacks, high-ranking black clergymen, and white philanthropists. James Forten, an affluent black sailmaker, supported the early conventions, as did Bishop Richard Allen, a founder of the African Methodist Episcopal Church. The Conventions' deliberations condemned slavery, of course, but always put greatest emphasis on conditions in the North, stressing self-help and protesting discrimination. The elite delegates made little headway, however, in establishing local conventions which could support their appeals. From 1835 to 1843, the National Convention failed to assemble, for its black leaders were temporarily caught up in the white immediatist cause.

By 1843, however, the movement was in the midst of a full revival, staffed by new leaders and supported by a wide network of auxiliaries. In this eight-year interval, the blacks had discovered their powerlessness in white abolitionism and had seen their goals and those of the American Anti-Slavery Society evolving in different directions. The need to revivify the separate convention movement was clear. During these years of full alliance with the whites, however, a new generation of black leaders had begun to assert itself in local organizations. These men and women, often educated at places like Oberlin or Oneida Institute, were now directing their energies toward the revived Convention. James McCune Smith of New York City, Pennsylvanians John B. Vashon and Martin Delany, J. W. C. Pennington and Amos Beman of Hartford, and later, escapees like Frederick Douglass and Henry Highland Garnet were only some of the new participants who furnished the reborn Convention Movement with what it had lacked previously—managerial skill and a stable local and regional organization.

From the mid-1840's onward, the Convention Movement attempted to involve average black citizens directly in efforts to found schools, develop libraries, promote temperance, and battle discrimination. Later in the 1850's, disputes between Douglass, Delany, and others over the wisdom of black emigration shattered the national organization. Yet the state and local meetings continued to function through the end of the Civil War, when national leaders again reassembled. In the meantime, the Convention Movement provided a forum for black leaders to debate ideas, to share in a common race identity, and most of all, to develop measures to reduce the level of oppression. Theirs was a herculean task, and their persistence never yielded more than minimal rewards.

Convention leaders spent the most time and resources in attempts to improve the quality of black education. Programs of self-help were fruitless, argued Martin Delany, if black children did not receive education which fitted them for careers which produced goods and income. Here, indeed, was wise advice in an age of rapid capital expansion. Others, like Samuel Cornish, emphasized high-quality schooling as a socializing device for imparting to black children the firm moral values of the adult community. Seeking these several ends, blacks throughout the North responded to the Convention's call to establish local education groups for young people, like New York's Phoenix Society and the Philomatheon Society of Boston. Offering instruction in various trades, literature, and basic academic skills, these voluntary associations soon sprang up in Philadelphia, Pittsburgh, Cleveland, Cincinnati, and elsewhere.

White reformers proved financially supportive of ad hoc organizations such as these. But they became decidedly less so as black abolitionists struggled to develop separate colleges and manual-training schools. After an initial flurry of enthusiasm during the 1830's, influential Garrisonians expressed their unremitting hostility to the idea of separate

black colleges and worked assiduously to discourage potential contributors. Blacks, too, split on the question of
separation in education, with some leaders like William C.
Nell arguing that integrated schools did "mighty work in
uprooting prejudice." Others, like Delany, argued that
blacks should attend separate colleges and receive training
to serve their race's exclusive needs. Internal disagreements
were only exacerbated by unsought white opinions like
those of Maria Weston Chapman, who denounced all
separate academies as "obeisances to slavery."

Similar problems beset the black reformers as they
attempted with marginal success to establish a national
newspaper. Samuel Cornish and John B. Russwurm tried
first in 1827 by publishing *Freedom's Journal*, which lasted
only two years. Cornish began again in 1837, over Garrison's
loud opposition, by founding the *Colored American*, which
survived on meager readership until 1841. When Douglass
finally succeeded in permanently establishing the *North Star*
in 1847, it was only over loud objections from Boston
Garrisonians and thanks to the charity of Gerrit Smith.

Alongside these twin frustrations of white criticism and
charity lay the obvious problem of black apathy. Black
newspapers like Cornish's failed because not enough black
readers cared to, or could, support them. Once, back in
1831, Garrison's *Liberator* had survived largely because
Boston's blacks had supported it. Now Douglass's own
paper relied on whites for eighty percent of its readership.
As early as 1829, David Walker excoriated his fellow blacks
for their lack of concern, and he would not be the last to do
so. How could the white man's prejudices ever abate,
Walker asked, "when we are confirming [them] every day
by our *groveling, submissions* and *treachery?*" But Samuel
Ringgold Ward had a point, too, when he placed primary
responsibility for black disinterest on the intensity of white

racism which, he was certain, "discourages [a person's] efforts, damps his ardor, blasts his hopes and embitters his spirit." As in their relationships with whites, black abolitionists were compelled to determine the limits of activism among their own race. It is hardly surprising that they discovered most Northern blacks preoccupied with the day-to-day trials of impoverishment, demoralized by even the idea of advancing the entire race against the overwhelming forces which blighted the existence of each of them. Granting exceptions like David Walker, it is also little wonder that black abolitionism's leaders exemplified privilege—successful ministers, brilliant fugitive slaves who enjoyed a degree of white patronage, and young, well-educated agitator-intellectuals.

Though uncommitted to militant race solidarity, the black community did furnish its activist element with a strong and invaluable institution—its churches. Here, more than anywhere else, was where the black community turned for physical assistance, psychological support, and discerning leadership. Most white churches ("free churches" set up by white abolitionists in the 1840's were usually an exception) had been segregated long before the eighteenth century. By the 1790's, jim crow practices among the white Methodists had stimulated the appearance of two separate black denominations—the Bethel African Methodist Church and the African Methodist Episcopal Church. During the 1820's, black Baptists also formed a separate organization, and as the 1830's opened, every black population center of consequence supported several active congregations.

Reflecting the inclinations of their members, most churches did not participate openly in black abolitionism. Such was the case even though the African Methodist Episcopal Church barred slaveholders in 1816. Most congregations, however, carried out self-help projects and education programs as they were urged to by the National Convention Movement. Abolitionist or not, every properly conducted black church contributed to a sense of community consciousness and race pride. Most black ministers, however, judiciously avoided open association with abolitionism, emphasizing noncontroversial themes of salvation in their sermons, not the sin of slavery.

Yet the ministry furnished black abolitionism with most of its leaders and inspiration. Samuel D. Cornish, William Allen, Charles B. Ray, Peter Williams, Henry Highland Garnet, Theodore S. Wright, and Samuel Ringgold Ward all occupied pulpits in the Methodist or Baptist churches, and this list could be expanded greatly. Black religion in the North, moreover, often contained a pronounced evangelicalism, although these leaders were hardly receptive to the romantic utopianism of the white reformers' religion. Belief in human perfectionism comported little with their struggles against exploitation and exclusion. Instead, black evangelicalism most often supported black abolitionism through its emphasis on God's retributive justice, its stress on the brotherhood of all mankind, and its insistence on diligence and personal uprightness.

Black congregations promoted abolition in other ways as well. Churches, for example, served a function about which whites often knew little and in which they participated only secondarily—the protection of fugitive slaves. As Larry Gara has demonstrated, a white-sponsored "underground railroad" which efficiently spirited fugitives out of slavery existed only in the realm of myth. While prominent whites like Levi Coffin, Samuel J. May, and Gerrit Smith did provide temporary protection for an occasional runaway, it remained largely to the blacks to protect escapees from federal marshals. They did so, often by using churches and private homes as locations for vigilance societies and as temporary havens for runaways.

New York City's vigilance group, dominated by blacks and managed until 1840 by tenacious David Ruggles, served as a model for others which arose in many black communities. Before 1850 these groups occasionally greeted slave catchers with physical resistance, as in Detroit in 1833 when a group of outraged blacks assaulted a local sheriff who was detaining accused fugitives. Most, however, initially preferred nonviolent opposition. But after the passage of the 1850 Fugitive Slave Law which placed every Northern black in jeopardy, premeditated violence became far more commonplace. "The only way to make the fugitive slave law dead letter," Douglass once vowed, "is to make a half a dozen or more dead kidnappers." In the Jerry McHenry rescue, blacks and whites shared some of Douglass's militancy and joined on several other occasions to rescue captives from the federal "bloodhounds."

Yet most who escaped slavery had only themselves and their fellow blacks to thank. Harriet Tubman, herself a fugitive who operated from Canada, reputedly made more than a dozen forays into the South and brought back more than two hundred people. In Pennsylvania, William Still also engineered slave escapes. Much more commonly, however, successful runaways relied on their own wits and the help of friendly slaves to escape from the "cotton kingdom." Once in the North, vigilance groups would then either settle fugitives in relatively safe surroundings or assist them through the free states to Canada where numerous escapees had already settled. Whites knew little, whatever the destination. James G. Birney once remarked that he knew "nothing" of these matters "generally until they are passed."

White abolitionists did not, however, ignore the plight of

the fugitives. Charles Turner Torrey, for one, suffered a martyr's fate, dying in a Maryland jail cell after being convicted of abetting escaped slaves. Captain Daniel Drayton also went to prison for attempting to spirit slaves out of Washington, D.C., in the hold of his merchant ship. Yet such instances were exceptional, and in Torrey's case it is likely that his actions reflected a pathological desire for martyrdom. In any case, white abolitionists usually took deepest interest in fugitives who, like Douglass, were eager to testify to the horrors of slavery. Here were the most authentic witnesses of all, far superior even to former slaveholders like Birney. White audiences turned out in large numbers to hear daring black speakers describe what their lives had been like under the peculiar institution.

In this age of romantic sentimentalism, fugitive slaves turned public speakers made perhaps the most effective black contribution of all to the crusade against slavery. Henry Bibb could move audiences to weeping as he recounted how his wife, naked and bound, had been whipped by her brutal master. The white response to Ellen Craft, a striking, light-skinned fugitive, was no less emotional, but more revealing. "To think of such a woman being held as a piece of property," exclaimed the white Garrisonian Samuel May, Jr. That so fair-complected and, to whites, so attractive a black person was "subject to be traded off to the highest bidder (while in reality no worse than when done to the blackest woman that ever was)" touched even the most prejudiced souls, May believed.

By the 1840's, Douglass, William Wells Brown, Samuel Ringgold Ward, Harriet Tubman, William and Ellen Craft, Sojourner Truth, and many other escaped slaves had taken to lecturing throughout the North. Their narrations of physical abuse and privation, of separation from loved ones, of emotional distress, forced whites to remember the conditions faced daily by over two million people still enslaved. Yet as May's comments regarding Ellen Craft indicate, black fugitive-activists constantly faced the problem of being viewed by whites as useful theatrical exhibits. When Douglass was refining his rhetorical skills, members of the American Anti-Slavery Society feared for his authenticity, since he now appeared too "learned." "People won't believe you were ever a slave, Frederick," Garrison warned. Parker Pillsbury added that it was "better [to] have a *little* of the plantation manner of speech than not." This white manipulation almost always accompanied the assistance so necessary in launching careers like Douglass's.

And often there was no question of the need for aid. Wealthy, literate, commanding the lecture circuits, and enjoying full access to the printing press, the white reformers' capacity to help the careers of fugitive-activists was obvious. White abolitionists commonly collaborated with fugitives, editing or ghostwriting their slave narratives and then subsidizing publication. William Wells Brown, for example, requested Edmund Quincy, a white Garrisonian, to edit his manuscript. White abolitionists in turn were anxious that these narratives be factually correct, for by the mid-1840's slave memoirs had achieved a tremendous readership. Douglass's *Autobiography* (written without assistance) sold widely in 1850.

These narratives gave Northern whites a comprehensive picture of life in slavery, one which controverted easy stereotype with brutal reality. Accompanying the commonly rehearsed themes of mistreatment were emphatic portraits of stable black families, presided over by resourceful men and women who acquired skills, built institutions, and satisfied material needs on their own. In the past decade, in fact, historians have confirmed the accuracy of these narratives, using them with other kinds of data to begin the historical reconstruction of black culture in American slavery. By stressing the slaves' humanity, their cultural vitality, and their accomplishments, slave narratives thus confuted prevailing racial myths.

Considering the extent of racism, however, it is hardly surprising that feelings of alienation against all of white society surfaced early among black abolitionists. The men who revived the National Convention Movement in 1843 did so after sensing the inadequacy of white reform. Another much more ominous symptom of estrangement was the increasing willingness of powerful spokesmen like Henry Highland Garnet and Samuel Ringgold Ward to invoke the memory of Nat Turner. Indeed, at the 1843 convention Garnet delivered "An Address to the Slaves of the United States of America" which urged rebellion against the masters. Frederick Douglass and Charles Remond opposed Garnet's call, but largely on expedient grounds— revolt in the South would further jeopardize free blacks everywhere. By 1849, Douglass had changed his position, announcing that he would welcome the news of insurrection. In the next year black leaders moved further toward violence, responding to the Fugitive Slave Law by vowing to resist the slave catchers with force. Vigilance societies multiplied and reissued David Walker's *Appeal*; intrepid men like Garnet carried side arms.

In black circles during the 1850's, endorsements of defensive and revolutionary violence thus transformed alienation into a far different attitude. This "siege mentality" expressed itself most forcefully in espousals of black nationalism and proposals for emigration. The origins of antebellum black nationalism can be traced to the 1830's to the ideas of Lewis Woodson, an early preceptor of Martin Delany. Emigrationist projects developed by blacks also date to an earlier time, 1815, when shipowner Paul Cuffe sent thirty-eight free blacks to Sierra Leone. Yet until the 1850's, most black leaders equated emigration with the hated American Colonization Society. Nationalism had also been a minor theme in black ideology. Once the new Fugitive Slave Law took force, however, some nine thousand Northern blacks immediately fled to Canada. Soon after, emigrationists began holding national conventions. Besides debating the merits of moving to Haiti, the Gold Coast, or Mexican California, they emphasized their conviction that reform within the United States was impossible. Now, they stressed, the destiny of the black race lay in building a new and just civilization, one which would war against the African slave trade and all forms of inherited servitude.

By the late 1850's many black spokesmen, but especially Garnet, Ward, and Alexander Crummell, were involved in emigrationism. Even Douglass, who normally stood foursquare for continuing the struggle on American soil, investigated the possibility of founding an emigrant colony in Haiti. It was Martin Delany, however, who emerged as emigrationism's most serious proponent. A Harvard-educated physician, Delany supported emigrationism by an intense identification with black revolutionaries of the past, especially Nat Turner, Denmark Vesey, and Toussaint L'Ouverture. In his incomplete novel manuscript, *Blake*, the central character is a black guerrilla warrior, kidnapped from Cuba into the Deep South. There Blake foments revolt, encouraged by associates who live in the memory of Nat Turner's stirring days and know that racial unity is the vital ingredient of successful revolution. Delany himself, spurred by these visions and convinced that the destiny of all blacks lay in Africa, led an expedition up the Niger River in 1859, mapping likely sites for settlement.

Nothing permanent came of Delany's efforts, however,

and after 1861 espousals of emigration and nationalism temporarily ceased. War and emancipation rekindled in the black abolitionists a hope that white America was susceptible to reform. The significance of the militancy of the 1850's lies not in projects completed or revolutions begun. In Delany's specific plans as in the general endorsements of black exodus, alienation had crystallized into a sweeping ideology that transcended national identity. Considering the frustrations which could drive blacks so completely away from white abolitionism, it is noteworthy that the two groups joined forces as often as they did.

Black and white reformers discovered very early that collaboration was easiest and most effective in campaigns to combat legal and customary discrimination. Indeed, in their challenges to segregated public schools, jim crow public accommodations, and legislative disenfranchisement, the whites' romantic penchant for moral rectitude and the blacks' practical goal of mitigating oppression harmonized nicely. Whites like Parker Pillsbury who burned to bear witness to "truth" could work alongside blacks like Frederick Douglass whose vital interest was in easing caste oppression as best they could. An incident during the summer of 1841 in New Bedford, Massachusetts, reveals how the process worked.

It began in June when David Ruggles, the militant director of the New York City vigilance committee, refused to sit in the "blacks only" section of a steamer bound for Nantucket. The next month Ruggles was back, this time boarding the "white car" of the New Bedford railway. After being dragged from the car, Ruggles took the railway to court, and local blacks threatened antidiscrimination suits. The judge, however, held in favor of the railroad, whereupon Garrison and his white friends rushed to New Bedford to denounce the decision. On August 9, the editor of the

Liberator took it upon himself to organize a protest meeting.

The next day Garrison and Douglass, along with forty other black and white abolitionists, boarded a steamer from which Ruggles had also been ejected. On this particular day the captain relented, and the integrated group climbed up to the open-air "Negro deck" to enjoy the sunshine and hold an antislavery meeting, complete with speeches and resolutions condemning segregation. It was a pleasant outing, and the "two abolitionisms" had indeed reinforced one another nicely. Soon individual acts of civil disobedience as well as concerted efforts by integrated groups became common throughout New England.

These protests were not always so cheerfully nonviolent however. Blacks who entered the "whites only" sections of public conveyances invited treatment that whites who defied segregation usually escaped. In Lynn, Massachusetts, Mary Green, holding a baby, was dragged out of a "whites only" railroad car, struck, and hurled to the ground. Her husband, daring to intervene, received a beating. White abolitionists usually experienced this sort of handling only when accompanied by black associates. When Wendell Phillips and Nathaniel P. Rogers boarded segregated trains alone or with other whites, conductors sullenly pretended not to notice.

In our age where theoretical equality under the law remains controverted by the brutal reality of discrimination, it is tempting to dismiss a long-ago victory over segregated transportation in Massachusetts as devoid of enduring significance. Yet, to be freed from the cramped, rancid "nigger" railway cars was to be liberated from experiences of group debasement and self-hate. Such a dismissal also overlooks the fact that most abolitionists, whatever their race, understood their boycotts, lawsuits, and acts of civil disobedience as integral to moral suasion—public appeals which transcended local issues and confronted the white North with its racism. One can only speculate on what the quality of American race relations might have been if such agitation had been absent from our history.

At the time, however, abolitionists often struggled against degrading separatism because desegregation held out the important promise of better education for young people in the North. In some states like Ohio and Illinois, which legislated against blacks in public education, activists of both races raised funds to establish private schools. In some cases, black children and white did try to mingle in the same classrooms, but physical abuse and educational disaster were the only visible results. In such situations, many black parents requested segregated facilities and then agitated constantly for their improvement. But most often, black and white abolitionists joined forces in boycotts, lawsuits, and civil disobedience with school desegregation as their immediate goal.

During the 1840's, local blacks often successfully boycotted segregated schools and received considerable assistance from whites. White Garrisonians participated openly in a boycott in Nantucket, Massachusetts, while in Salem the former mayor, Stephen C. Phillips, an influential Conscience Whig, also sided with the boycotters there. In Rochester, Douglass enlisted his white colleagues in protracted battles which technically ended separate and unequal black public schools in that city.

The most significant desegregation struggles in public education centered in Boston and transpired over a decade, and brought together some of the antislavery crusade's already famous whites and previously obscure blacks. The conflict in Boston took root in 1829 when the mayor purposely neglected to invite a fully deserving black honors student, William C. Nell, to a city-sponsored banquet recognizing outstanding seniors. By the mid-1840's, Nell repaid the insult by leading a protracted campaign to integrate Boston's schools. Inspired by the success of the Salem boycott in 1844, Nell enlisted another black abolitionist whose children attended segregated schools, John T. Hilton, and together they began a petition campaign directed at the Boston school committee. When petitions failed, boycotts began, stimulated by the discovery that one of the white teachers in an all-black school enjoyed administering excessive punishments and was habitually absent from class.

Horace Mann, secretary of the Massachusetts Board of Education, tried without success to engineer compromise, while school authorities continued to reject the petitions of Nell's Friends of Equal School Rights Society. When Mann tried to ease the situation by appointing a new black principal to replace a white in one of the segregated schools, Nell and Hilton called forth black parents, surrounded the school, and attempted to prevent students from registering. Police drove them away from the schoolyard and the black principal took office, but the boycott of segregated schools remained in force until April 1855. In that year the state government finally outlawed all distinctions of color and religion in Massachusetts schools. Eleven years of black persistence had resulted in the first statewide desegregation decision in American history. Black leaders had dominated throughout, and white abolitionists had proven their worth as loyal supporters, not patronizing critics.

The boycotts had involved the desegregation effort in two expensive court suits. Here was the arena in which white expertise proved most valuable to black abolitionism. In 1849, for example, black attorney Robert Morris and Massachusetts' leading Free-Soiler, Charles Sumner, developed a lawsuit, known as the Roberts Case, against the

Boston school committee's segregationist policies. Appealing adverse lower-court rulings before the State Supreme Court in 1850, Sumner and Morris argued without success most of the grounds which were to be adopted by the plaintiffs one hundred four years later in the 1954 *Brown v. Board of Education of Topeka* desegregation suit. On many similar occasions, other white attorneys such as Salmon P. Chase put their services at the disposal of blacks ensnared by the North's highly prejudiced legal system. Here again, just as in the sit-ins and boycotts, the "two abolitionisms" interacted without friction to benefit the cause. Sectional figures of high standing found opportunity to express genuine humanitarian concern while trumpeting their opposition to the "slave power's" mastery of American law. Black defendants, fortunate to be expertly represented, at least had a better chance to receive a fair hearing.

In 1848 Frederick Douglass attended the Buffalo convention of the Free-Soil Party, hoping for the nomination of John P. Hale. Surrounded by racist Van Burenites like David Wilmot, dedicated reformers like Joshua Leavitt, and sincere but partial friends of black freedom like Edward Wade, his feelings of ambivalence must have been strong. The New York Liberty men in attendance, original immediatists like Leavitt, Henry B. Stanton, and Alvan Stewart, had campaigned hard in that state's referendum two years earlier to remove restrictions on the right of blacks to vote—just one among many instances when white Liberty men had supported efforts to repeal laws against blacks. Nevertheless, white supremacy was rapidly emerging as a central feature of political antislavery. Van Buren's presence testified to that, as did warnings from haughty Maria Weston Chapman and other patronizing Garrisonians that antiblack expedience permeated all the cries for "free soil." Nevertheless, Douglass could see one thing absolutely clearly: The power to free the slaves lay in the rough-and-tumble of racist free-soil politics, not in the salons of Beacon Hill Garrisonians. Ultimately, Douglass hoisted the name of Martin Van Buren to the masthead of his *North Star*.

7

Abolitionists and the Coming of the Civil War

Early in 1857 William Lloyd Garrison and John Brown met for the only time in Theodore Parker's home. Though Parker and Garrison were unaware of the fact, it had been at Brown's hands in Kansas six months earlier that five unarmed settlers had been brutally murdered in the dead of night—shot, then stabbed with swords, their bodies left along Pottawotamie Creek. Since 1854, the struggle between free-staters and slavery men over the destiny of Kansas had already claimed the lives of pioneers who had settled there as free-soilers. In murdering five emigrants from the slave states, Brown had envisioned himself God's bloody avenger, commissioned to correct the scales of justice. Little wonder that Brown and Garrison could find no agreement as they debated one of Garrison's favorite topics—Christian nonresistance. Each time Garrison referred to the pacifism of Jesus, Brown, inwardly sneering at such "milk and water" abolitionism, countered with the bloody prophecies of Jeremiah.

In the years immediately following the Compromise of 1850, until 1854 at least, such violent developments would have been hard to predict. The Compromise, accepted grudgingly at first by many political spokesmen, quickly became the object of rhetorical veneration. Shaken by their recent flirtations with sectional holocaust, politicians everywhere vowed that Henry Clay's package of concessions constituted a "final solution" to slavery questions. Events seemed to bear out this view. In every Northern state during the early 1850's, the Free-Soil Party began to fall apart, merging its organizations with one or the other of the two major parties in exchange for offices and programs. An independent Free-Soil Party did compete in the 1852 presidential contest, with John P. Hale as its candidate, but its vote was small and its impact on the election was minimal as Democrat Franklin Pierce overwhelmed the Whig's Winfield Scott. By 1853, an organized antislavery third party was all but absent from politics.

Equally cheering to slaveholders and sectionally bipartisan Northerners was the renewed interest displayed by many Yankees in holding Unionist meetings and in mobbing abolitionists. In New York City, for example, businessmen and merchants organized a Union Safety Committee to disrupt the May 1850 meeting of the American Anti-Slavery Society and to express solidarity with their business associates in the slave states. In Tammany Hall ward-heeler Isaiah Rynders, these "gentlemen of property and standing" found a person able and eager to mobilize the antiabolitionist lower-class Irish of New York. The abolitionists attempted to convene at the Broadway Tabernacle, harassments began, someone threatened to cut off Charles C. Burleigh's luxuriant curls, and Rynders's bullies stormed the rostrum. True to their principles of nonresistance, the Garrisonians did nothing to defend themselves. It seemed to some conservatives like a return to the more placid days of the early 1830's: abolitionists reduced to a noisy handful, no seriously disruptive anti-Southern third party in national elections, Whigs and Democrats competing for office on sectionally noncontroversial issues. Yet a more misleading conclusion than this is hard to imagine. Despite appearances, anti-Southern feeling continued to spread in the Northern wings of both parties during the early 1850's.

As Free-Soil leaders jockeyed with Whigs and Democrats in the state legislatures during the early 1850's, nonvoting Garrisonians kept up their now-traditional stream of criticism, inveighing against third-party adherents for their willingness to compromise. Political abolitionists like Gamaliel Bailey, now editor of the influential, Washington-based *National Era*, once again gave general support to these coalition maneuvers, but pressed the Free-Soilers not to lose sight of higher antislavery goals. But whether the abolitionists approved or not, it was clear that the Free-Soilers' bargains with the major parties during the late 1840's and early 1850's brought significant gains for political antislavery. Sectional politics was developing a momentum of its own, apart from abolitionist activity. In the process, these coalitions with Free-Soilers only made the Whigs and Democrats even more vulnerable to sectional disruption than they had been prior to the 1850 Compromise. Quietly now, even in the absence of dramatic conflict in Washington, divisive sectional forces continued to eat away at the traditional two-party system.

In Massachusetts, for example, a famous series of coalitions between Free-Soilers and Democrats sent to the United States Senate elegant Charles Sumner, widely noted for his bombast against slaveholding and his courtroom attacks on segregation. "By the license of slavery," he once declared on the Senate floor, "a whole race is delivered over to prostitution and concubinage, without the protection of any law." Always a close friend of nonvoters like Wendell

Phillips and Edmund Quincy and a confidant of Theodore Parker, Sumner was also a devoted reader of the *Liberator*. He also maintained close ties with old antislavery congressmen like Joshua Giddings and with such Liberty Party men turned Free-Soilers as Gamaliel Bailey, Salmon P. Chase, and Joshua Leavitt. Indeed, one can see in Sumner's 1851 election to the Senate a telling sign of antislavery consensus and a portent of the wrenching sectional divisions to come. In Ohio, meanwhile, a Whig–Free Soil coalition during 1851 allowed another great pocket of antislavery constituents to elect a senator. In that year, the two parties combined to launch Benjamin Wade's career as a blunt-spoken foe of the "slave power." In 1849, Free-Soil cooperation with the Democrats had elected Salmon P. Chase as senator.

Calling themselves Independent Democrats, Free Democrats, or Free-Soil Whigs, these new senators constituted only one measure of how steadily Northern politics continued to sectionalize after the crisis of 1850. Such terms as Free Democrat and Free-Soil Whig further indicated that many Northern Whigs and Democrats, voters as well as leaders, now made opposition to the "slave power" a prerequisite of continuing allegiance. In this fashion, the Whigs and Democrats were able for a while longer to perpetuate their solidarity. Yet even the many Northern officeholders who continued to worship, in historian Joel Silby's phrase, at the "shrine of party," did so by repeating in their ceremonies stern anathemas upon the "slave power." So although it appeared placid to conservatives, the atmosphere surrounding the American party system became increasingly volatile. One additional shock just might touch off violent upheaval. Meanwhile, many root-and-branch abolitionists began to contrive direct confrontations with the government. Instead of denying the moral authority of the United States government on radical nonresistance grounds, as had most Garrisonian disunionists, increasing numbers of abolitionists of all persuasions now began to condone physical resistance to unjust law.

Nearly thirty years earlier, abolitionists had entertained very different opinions about the use of violence. The original immediatists of the 1830's had organized as forthrightly nonviolent, promoting moral suasion rather than coercive means. At the time, their choice had been wise as well as logical. Peaceful tactics had harmonized with the broader tenets of evangelical reform from which abolitionism had drawn so much of its inspiration. Besides, a number of early immediatists, especially Quakers, had possessed abiding commitments to nonviolence. Indeed, nonviolence had been one of the critical elements of the abolitionists' original radicalness. In an age which exalted the political manipulator, favored the slaveowner, and condoned the mob, abolitionists had depended instead on peaceful appeals to conscience. But immediatists had also adopted pacifism for obvious tactical reasons. Founded in an atmosphere ridden with fear of slave revolts, the American Anti-Slavery Society had been well advised to make clear its abhorrence of black insurrection. Moreover, as a despised minority surrounded by powerful proslavery institutions, abolitionists had been dictated by prudence as well as principle in responding passively to mob assault. Until the 1850's, any widespread attempt by abolitionists to promote violence quite likely would have called down a wave of unparalleled repression. As Merton Dillon has observed, however, persons who had come to embrace nonviolence for these largely practical reasons could obviously discard the tactic whenever changes in circumstances or personal frustration seemed to warrant so doing. For some abolitionists, the events of the 1850's appeared to offer ample reasons indeed.

Many abolitionists also carried into the 1850's other attitudes, apart from these tactical concerns, which predisposed them to accept and practice violence. One of these was the Biblical emphasis on God's bloody vengeance for the sin of slavery. Another was the experience of the Liberty Party itself. Garrisonian nonresistants had cautioned third-party organizers from the outset that to manipulate politics directly was in itself an acceptance of coercive means different only in degree from the use of force. Indeed, even zealous nonresistants like Henry C. Wright, Stephen S. Foster, Parker Pillsbury, and finally, William Lloyd Garrison could accommodate their principles to calls for violent revolution. As Lewis Perry has cogently explained, nonresistance theories contained "intellectual loopholes" which allowed their proponents to endorse bloody deeds. Their religious radicalism, in short, gave way to simple extremism. Foster, for example, spoke as a sincere nonresistant when announcing that "every man should act on his own convictions, whether he believed in using moral or physical force." Hence, Foster argued, he himself was free to urge others to kill the kidnappers of fugitive slaves and to call the slaves to arms.

But early in the new decade, many abolitionists also found that their own memories, their assessments of nearly two decades of struggle, were provoking them to violence. Twenty years of preaching the sin of slavery had witnessed, not emancipation, but an increase of over four hundred thousand black people held in bondage. It was no less discouraging to realize that, despite their arduous, endless espousals of "moral revolution," the area of the slave states had continued to expand, automatically guaranteeing the growth of the "slave power" in all aspects of American life. At the same time, the boundaries of America's moral sensitivity could seem to have narrowed proportionately.

Liberty men such as James G. Birney and Gerrit Smith, recalling their earnest efforts early in the 1840's to make the electoral process serve humanity, now shuddered at the results. Political abolitionism, as an independent force in politics, seemed to have taken a downward course from the halcyon days of the "one idea" emancipationist platform, through the Free-Soil compromise with the Van Burenites, to near extinction. Birney's disillusion drove him into bitter seclusion in the Michigan wilderness whence he counseled all blacks to flee the United States. Smith found solace in the "political antipolitics" of the Liberty League, in making donations to John Brown's Kansas enterprises, and in defying the Fugitive Slave Law. Ann Greene Phillips perhaps best summed up a feeling of desperation which was fast overtaking many abolitionists: "We may as well disband at once, if our meetings and papers are all talk and we never do anything *but talk.*"

Symbolizing all that was reprehensible in the nation's continuing compromise with evil, the new Fugitive Slave Law became the primary target of abolitionist resistance throughout the 1850's. From the moment of its enactment, abolitionists and antislavery politicians emphasized their grim determination to oppose it—by force, if necessary. *"We cannot be Christians and obey it,"* Giddings warned bluntly. Hard-bitten black abolitionists like Samuel Ringgold Ward had long ago concluded that "the right and duty of the oppressed to destroy their oppressors" was demanded by "God's Holy Writ." But abolitionist Samuel J. May had an impressive record of Christian pacifism. It is therefore significant that he, like Giddings and Ward, told his parishioners in 1851 that they were under Holy "obligation" to defy the law, just "as you are not to lie, steal and murder."

As opposition to the Fugitive Slave Law satisfied some of

the abolitionists' urges for direct action, it also began to submerge them ever more completely in the broader Northern struggles against the "slave power." The many estrangements which usually separated evangelicals from anticlericals, Free-Soil Whigs and Free Democrats from Liberty Leaguers, and black abolitionists from whites vanished as Northerners explored yet another level of antislavery consensus. Unlike other occasions in American history, these acts of defiance against the state did not touch off a wave of repression against an isolated radical fringe or stimulate abrupt turns in the public's attitude toward conservatism. Instead, abolitionists discovered that the more strident they made their opposition to the law, the more widespread became Northern resentment against the "slave power."

Long before 1850, abolitionists had made good on pledges to aid fugitives, regardless of the original 1793 Law. Whites had helped while blacks organized vigilance societies, harassed sheriffs, and relocated escapees. Anger at Northern involvement in slave-hunting was hardly new either, as the personal-liberty laws passed in various states attested. What was new after 1850 was the intensity and pervasiveness of Northern resistance. A new generation of Beechers— Charles and Henry Ward, sons of the old evangelical colossus Lyman Beecher—led a host of eloquent young ministers like Methodist Gilbert Haven and Presbyterian George B. Cheever, who preached of "higher laws" than those of Congress to which the practicing Christian owed first allegiance. Meanwhile, ministers like Samuel J. May, Theodore Parker, and Thomas Wentworth Higginson furnished examples of "practical Christianity" by engaging in public acts of noncompliance.

As we have seen, May was instrumental in the forcible

liberation of Jerry McHenry from the Syracuse jail. Still claiming to uphold nonviolence, he nevertheless expressed to Garrison feelings which other nonresistants were coming to share: "When I saw poor Jerry in the hands of the official kidnappers, I could not preach nonresistance very earnestly to the crowd who were clamoring for his release." In 1850, Parker, who never claimed to be a nonresistant, took command of the Boston vigilance committee, which now included Higginson, Wendell Phillips, Samuel Gridley Howe, and the black escapee Lewis Hayden. In 1851 the muscular Hayden led a group of blacks into a Boston courtroom and forcibly rescued a much-surprised fugitive Fred Wilkins (locally known as Shadrach). Parker, ecstatic, praised the deed as the "noblest done in Boston since the destruction of the tea." Higginson, who was also running for Congress at the time as a Free-Soil Democrat, likewise defended publicly Hayden's recourse to force. In September 1851, when a group of blacks in Christiana, Pennsylvania, fatally shot a federal marshal who attempted to seize one of their number, Parker called with enthusiasm for more such scenes.

Yet the fugitive-slave incident which probably illustrates most clearly the increasing coalescence of antislavery forces involved Thomas Sims. Sims, an escapee from Georgia, was seized by marshals after a fierce struggle in April 1851. The Boston vigilance committee convened hurriedly, and non-resistants like Garrison contributed pacifist suggestions as Phillips, Parker, Higginson, and Hayden considered various strategies for freeing the captive. Meanwhile, as one hundred fifty policemen surrounded the courthouse in which Sims was held, antislavery politicians came forward to seek Sims's release through legal appeals. Among them were Samuel Sewall, founding member of the American

Anti-Slavery Society and later a Liberty man, Free Democrat Robert Rantoul, and Conscience Whig turned Free
Democrat Charles Sumner.

Protest meetings were simultaneously called for, and
sectional figures of nearly every description eagerly attended. Horace Mann, now a Free-Soil Whig congressman,
presided over the meeting in Tremont Temple, and Samuel
Gridley Howe, a vigilance committee member predisposed
to violence, convened the meeting. The speakers included
the old immediatist Elizur Wright, Jr., the aspiring Free-Soil
politician Henry Wilson, and two apostles of force—the
disunionist Wendell Phillips and the radical minister-politi-
cian Thomas Wentworth Higginson. Some counseled law
and order, but Higginson, with "fire in the eye," made his
listeners tremble with his calls for violent resistance. "We
were on the eve of revolution with that speech," Phillips
recalled.

That the gathering ultimately endorsed a due regard for
law and order in no way diminishes a far more important
fact: Antislavery politicians and abolitionists of all shadings
were openly opposing federal authority, debating the limits
of peaceful dissent, and exploring the imperatives of forcible
resistance. In the process, immediatist radicals were becoming increasingly difficult to distinguish from sectionally
aroused politicians; their functions as reformers became
ever more restricted to their ability to add to the atmosphere of sectional crisis. For example, when all his legal
appeals had failed, the lawyer-politician Charles Sumner
agreed with the vigilance committee's last, desperate (and
unworkable) plan to intercept and forcibly board the slave
ship which was to transport Sims back to Georgia.

Despite the commotion generated by acts of resistance,
the Fugitive Slave Law was never rendered unenforceable,
as scholars once claimed. In parts of New England, in

upstate New York, and in the Western Reserve, to be sure, the law was openly flouted and fugitives were received with great ceremony. In April 1859, for example, when some daring federal marshals ventured into Oberlin and seized a fugitive slave, a mob of students, faculty, and irate towns-folk immediately rescued the captive and were later acquitted by a local jury. Yet on many occasions, escapees were quickly arrested before local antislavery forces had a chance to prevent it. In some areas, especially in southern Ohio, Indiana, Illinois, and Pennsylvania, abolitionist leadership was often nonexistent, and citizens complied willingly with the marshals. Furthermore, as the abortive efforts to rescue Thomas Sims demonstrated, policemen and magistrates could provide the marshals with considerable support. Most formidable, however, to the "foes of the slave power" was the obvious determination of President Franklin Pierce (a New Hampshire man) to enforce the law with massive federal power.

Logically, Pierce chose Boston as the site for his display of federal authority. On May 25, 1854, a well-educated young fugitive named Anthony Burns was arrested, the first in Boston since Thomas Sims. Again the vigilance committee convened, the protest meetings assembled, and Phillips and Parker all but urged violent action to end Burns's captivity. Suddenly a cry rang out that hundreds of men, led by Higginson, were storming the courthouse; they threw bricks, battered down the front door, and rushed inside to seek Anthony Burns. Instead, they confronted the court-house guards, and during the height of the melee one guard was fatally shot. Immediately the police arrived and began arresting rioters. Upon their request for federal troops, the police received a telegram from Pierce: "Your conduct is approved. The law must be executed." Several days later Higginson, now himself a fugitive from an arrest warrant, mounted the pulpit to announce: "I can only make my life worth living for, by becoming a revolutionist." Yet he was no more able to aid Burns than were the Garrisonian nonresistants who had expressed dismay at Higginson's violent comportment. All the armed forces which could be mustered in Boston lined the route from the courthouse to the wharf as Burns, surrounded by marshals, was led to the ship which returned him to the South.

Stark in its drama, frightening in its implications, the specter of armed federal troops occupying the streets of Boston against its own "freedom-loving" citizens greatly increased long-standing Northern fears of the "slave power's" intentions. Pierce's role (like Jackson's antiabolitionism in the 1830's) suggested strongly that the office of the president itself, the army he commanded, the powers of executive order and veto he enjoyed, the party system that supported him, had now been placed at the exclusive disposal of the planter class. Northerners in both major parties wondered increasingly whether any civil liberties remained under firm guarantee, or whether republicanism existed at all apart from the generosity of the planter class. Men like Parker challenged their audiences: "We are the vassals of Virginia. It reaches its arm over the graves of our mothers, it kidnaps men in the city of Puritans, over the graves of Samuel Adams and John Hancock." Moved by precisely these feelings, Garrison endowed his oft-declared disunionism with a new, more bellicose tone. On July 4, 1854, in Framingham, Massachusetts, he ceremoniously burned first a copy of the Fugitive Slave Law, then a copy of the court decision which ordered Anthony Burns's reenslavement, and finally a copy of the American Constitution. The abolitionists who looked on cheered wildly. While moderate antislavery men and women often deplored Garrison's "excesses," all sectionally sensitive Northerners nevertheless understood clearly the symbolism of his ritual. The gap which most antislavery supporters had for so long claimed as separating them from abolitionist extremism narrowed accordingly.

Theodore Parker and others spoke as revolutionaries and counseled defiance of federal statute. But as his remarks indicate, Parker's appeal for resistance invoked the most venerable of American traditions. Many who flouted the law and courted violence saw themselves moved by the ideals of the American Revolution. By emulating the Sons of Liberty, they envisioned themselves reasserting the very principles of freedom for which their grandfathers had presumably fought. Throughout the 1850's, Phillips constantly invoked the memories of Crispus Attucks and Sam Adams as he urged his listeners to greet the federal marshals as the Patriots had welcomed the Redcoats on Lexington Green. Likewise availing himself of the Revolution's precedent, Joshua Giddings organized in his home county a vigilance committee, the Sons of Liberty, which was dedicated to meeting slave catchers with lethal force if need be.

Slaveholders noted that political mavericks and third-party ideologues like Giddings, Henry Wilson, Horace Mann, and Charles Sumner were joining in protests with unabashed radical abolitionists like Phillips and Parker and felt reconfirmed in their deepest, most frightening suspicions. Despite their disavowals of immediatism, what distinguished these Free-Soil politicians from the most extravagant Garrisonians? Free-Soilers claimed to oppose only the westward progress of slavery; yet how did their militant appeals to "higher law" and their invitations to "irrepressible conflict" differ from the intentions of a Gerrit Smith? Besides, was it not apparent to Sumner and the rest that to arrest the expansion of slavery was to force the South into moral capitulation, inviting social upheaval?

Seen from the plantation, Benjamin Wade, John P. Hale, and Horace Mann thus appeared no less genuine abolitionists than did members of the American Anti-Slavery Society. Yet Northern Whigs and Democrats seemed eager to deal with these partisans and even created senatorships for Wade, Sumner, Salmon P. Chase, and Hannibal Hamlin. Was such behavior evidence that the Northern branches of the two parties were falling victim to abolitionist madness? During the early 1850's, increasing numbers of planters acted on just such suspicions. Soon they began pressing for stronger safeguards, once again demanding access to Western lands which would guarantee the political dominance of slavery within the Union.

Next to John Brown and his sons, the family most responsible for heightening these Southerners' anxieties was undoubtedly the Beechers. Ever since the mid-1830's, all but Catherine Beecher had made their family name synonymous with clerical abolitionism. Old Lyman Beecher, it will be remembered, had provoked family dissent in 1835 when he had attempted to mollify the Lane Seminary rebels. Two years later in Alton, Illinois, Lyman's oldest son, Edward Beecher, had mounted a vocal defense of abolitionism as Elijah P. Lovejoy prepared to do battle with the mob. In 1850, as noted, two other sons, Henry Ward Beecher and Charles Beecher, preached noncompliance with the Fugitive Slave Law. Yet it was quiet Harriet Beecher, now married to Calvin Stowe, whose work proved the most unsettling of all to the planter class. In 1852 Gamaliel Bailey's *National Era* began weekly installments of her newly completed novel, *Uncle Tom's Cabin*. Even as abolitionists, politicians, and black runaways joined in resistance to the Fugitive Slave Law, literate people all over the North read avidly of the tribulations endured by Uncle

Tom, George and Eliza Harris, and the others during their years trapped in slavery.

A central event in the history of popular literature, *Uncle Tom's Cabin* made hostility to slavery routine expression in family entertainment. Throughout the North, impresarios set about inventing dances and orchestrating dramatic readings based on the book's plot. In the 1830's, abolitionism had appropriated the techniques of mass journalism; after 1852, hostility to the "slave power" permeated the carnival world of P. T. Barnum. Indeed, *Uncle Tom's Cabin* satisfied every antislavery taste. For nonresistants, there was ever-forgiving, ever-Christian Uncle Tom, meeting force with pious submission; for those attracted by violence, there was gun-wielding George Harris, the desperate fugitive; for activist women, Eliza Harris combined beauty, bravery, and independence with a fierce devotion to family and home; for racist Free-Soilers, there were Stowe's expressions of support for colonization and her racial stereotypes; for proponents of free labor who abhorred the planter class, there were Tom's first owners, Shelby and St. Clare, well-meaning but effeminate, dissipated and improvident, enervated by lives of slothful dependence on their bondsmen; and for Northerners who felt complicitous for whatever reason in maintaining the peculiar institution, there was Simon Legree, the Yankee slavetrader, unsurpassed by any slaveholder in his wanton brutality.

Stowe's sole contact with slavery had been a few hours spent on a Kentucky plantation. Slave narratives and Theodore D. Weld's *Slavery As It Is* had provided her only background information. What Stowe did command, however, was an exact sense of Northern Protestant culture—its evangelical piety, its domesticity, its sentimentalism, its race prejudice, and, above all, its suspicion of the ways of the plantation. The book could not be printed fast enough to satisfy Northern demands. In the first year after publication, over three hundred thousand copies had been sold in the United States alone. In England *Uncle Tom's Cabin* sold over a million copies before 1861. White Southerners set about feverishly to rebut Stowe's work with hapless literary productions like *Aunt Phyllis's Cabin*.

But there was little that Southern whites could do to stop people in the North from reading what they chose. They also could not prevent the election of antislavery senators, suppress the incidents of defiance against the Fugitive Slave Law, or block the British efforts to stamp out slavery in Latin America. Slaveholders had but one recourse as they sought to guarantee the safety of their regime—to wrest further concessions from the North. Desperately aware of their numerical minority, fearing that "free-soil abolitionism" was making serious inroads in both parties, and sensing their shrinking base of political power, influential planters pressured Franklin Pierce and the Democratic Party leadership to open new Western lands to the expansion of slavery. In January 1854, Stephen A. Douglas sponsored a bill in Congress. He proposed to apply the doctrine of popular sovereignty in Kansas and Nebraska, opening to the possible expansion of slavery territories previously declared free as part of the 1820 Missouri Compromise.

What impelled Douglas to embrace so disruptive a course? Historians cite his burning presidential ambition which never could be satisfied without Southern support, his devotion to Western railroad projects, and his lack of appreciation for the electricity which surrounded slavery issues. Later he would remark that he cared little whether slavery was "voted up or down" in the territories. Yet Douglas surely knew from the beginning that his Kansas-Nebraska Bill would, as he put it, "raise a hell of a storm."

To him the storm seemed eminently worth braving if, through popular sovereignty, sectional disputes could be settled locally. National politics could then be forced back to its traditional principles of sectional bipartisanship and silence on slavery questions. Besides, he was certain that popular sovereignty would result in the peaceful creation of more new free states than slave states.

But these were vain hopes indeed, for sectional feelings had already penetrated the innermost recesses of the two-party system in the North. Douglas's bill destroyed the Whig Party entirely and grievously damaged the Northern Democrats. As Southern Whigs joined the Democrats in backing the Kansas-Nebraska Bill, Chase, Sumner, Giddings, Wade, and Gerrit Smith (who, through an unusual Liberty League–Free Soil coalition, had been elected to Congress) issued a forceful appeal to the voters of the North, warning of this "monstrous plot" to convert free territory into "a dreary region of despotism, inhabited by masters and slaves." Frontier lands once reserved by law for free white labor were now to be given as tribute to the insatiable "slave power," they warned. Editors and orators all over the North immediately embellished these themes, and the nation's political structure began to fragment and collapse. The demands of sectionalism were at last sapping the resilience of the two-party system. By late 1854, ex-Whigs, former Democrats, and Free-Soilers had come together, endorsing free soil and adopting the name of the Republican Party. The elements of an ultimate confrontation with the South had begun to fall into place. Abolitionists suddenly found themselves in the presence of a huge antislavery constituency.

By abolitionist standards, of course, this "moral revolution" in politics was partial, half-hearted, and blighted by an active, widespread hostility toward the black race. As the

Northern Whigs and anti-Nebraska Democrats united with Chase, Wade, Sumner, and Giddings against the Kansas-Nebraska Act, it was again clear that white supremacy, not racial tolerance, informed most of the renewed cry for "free soil, free labor, free men." Immediatists remained, in this important respect, well outside the limits of political orthodoxy. Yet, how were abolitionists to influence and provoke this greatly expanded antislavery coalition, at once so racially conservative, but so militant in resisting Southern demands? Obviously, older tactics such as third parties and disunionist agitation could no longer exert the influence that they had during the 1840's. As with the Northern resistance to the Fugitive Slave Law, the anti-Kansas-Nebraska movement clearly left abolitionists with a diminished sphere of action and more inclined to condone the violence that increasingly punctuated the sectional conflict.

And as it was, violence aplenty was in the offing. Once passed, the Kansas-Nebraska Act stimulated a footrace to the territories as free-staters and proslavery supporters struggled to control the elections which were to decide the territories' future by popular sovereignty. In Kansas, political struggle soon degenerated into guerrilla warfare, and many abolitionists welcomed the news of frontier bloodshed. Lydia Maria Child, usually an exemplar of pacifism, was outraged to learn that some free-staters had allowed themselves to be disarmed without a struggle by proslavery authorities. In Massachusetts, the old-line Whig textile merchant Amos A. Lawrence attempted to harness the popular anger over events in Kansas and move it in conservative directions. Accordingly, he underwrote the New England Emigrant Aid Company and the National Kansas Committee. These corporations, which recruited free-state settlers with offers of capital and rifles (called by some "Beecher's Bibles"), attracted the support of aboli-

tionist militants like Thomas Wentworth Higginson, Theodore Parker, Samuel Gridley Howe, and Wendell Phillips.
Once again radical abolitionists were being caught up in
broader violent trends. Charles B. Stearns, the roving
reporter for both the *Liberator* and *National Anti-Slavery
Standard* who believed in nonresistance, found himself in
Kansas in 1855 and immediately embraced the doctrine that
killing proslavery men was not in violation of his pacifist
creed. Most telling, however, were events that took place in
June 1855 when Gerrit Smith's Liberty Leaguers convened
in Syracuse for their annual meeting. Also present was John
Brown.

Smith, Frederick Douglass, Lewis Tappan, William
Goodell, and F. J. LeMoyne were the most prominent of
the long-standing abolitionists who listened as Brown appealed for aid in protecting Kansas free-staters. Brown left
the meeting with sixty dollars; thereafter he enjoyed
financial and moral support from many reform quarters.
Garrison, struggling to shore up the crumbling bastions of
nonresistance, dismissed the Kansas warriors as opportunists
and racists, while Lewis Tappan shuddered at reports of
Brown's massacre at Pottawotamie Creek. Tappan suggested that instead Kansas needed peaceful Christian missionaries, not "Beecher's Bibles."

Tappan and Garrison were clearly exceptions as abolitionists everywhere, some reluctantly, some with ardor,
supported the use of force. In days gone by, immediatists
had envisioned emancipation as a way to avoid race and
sectional violence; now many reformers, Garrisonians and
political abolitionists alike, invited such conflict. In the May
1857 meeting of the Massachusetts Anti-Slavery Society,
Henry C. Wright, still claiming zealous nonresistance,
argued that true abolitionists should furnish arms for slave
insurrections, and in this debate Wright enjoyed the full

support of Wendell Phillips. "I want to accustom Massachusetts to the idea of insurrection," Phillips declared, "to the
idea that every slave has the right to seize his freedom on
the spot." Garrison, his own mantle of nonresistance in
shreds, badgered the few remaining pacifists at the meeting
into silence. Clearly the cry "No Union with Slaveholders"
no longer satisfied these militant souls; yet disunion conventions, filled with violent rhetoric and sponsored by various
Garrisonians, still took place in Worcester and Cleveland
during 1857.

The direct political effect of these gatherings on other
Northerners was negligible and even negative, repelling
antislavery moderates with their extremist tone. Henry
Wilson, Charles Sumner, Joshua Giddings, and other militant Republicans publicly disavowed such violent espousals
and declined invitations to attend. Yet no matter how
diminished their distinctive voice in the Northern political
process had become, the abolitionists still exercised profound influence upon the South. Slaveholders marked the
disunion conventions and calls for slave insurrection grimly,
certain that in them were revealed the North's true
intentions, aims which Wilson, Salmon P. Chase, William H.
Seward, and Benjamin Wade would also support in mo-
ments of private candor.

But it was the white supremacist and proslavery dimensions of American politics after 1854 which most often
provoked thoughts of bloodshed in the minds of abolitionists. The fact that the Pierce administration, dominated by
planter interests, pursued blatantly proslavery policies in
Kansas only made it easier for abolitionists to justify
violence. After all, as Garrisonians and Liberty Leaguers
noted, Benjamin Wade, Henry Wilson, and Joshua Giddings
were only the most vocal of the Northern politicians who

urged Kansas free-staters to take up arms against the proslavery edicts of Franklin Pierce.

Indeed, on May 22, 1856, Wade and Wilson themselves could be seen stalking the halls of Congress, handguns bulging under their coats. Earlier that day, on the floor of the Senate, a South Carolina representative, Preston S. Brooks, had beaten Charles Sumner senseless with a heavy cane, avenging his family name for "insults" uttered by Sumner during the course of his speech on the "Crime of Kansas." Wade and Wilson muttered threats of vengeance, and even Northern conservatives like Edward Everett gasped at the daring brutality of the deed and reported that outrage at the slaveholders was now "deeper and more dangerous" than ever before. In Kansas, meantime, news of "bleeding Sumner" hastened the cycle of events which saw proslavery forces sack the free-soil town of Lawrence.

Meanwhile, all opponents of slavery, violently inclined or not, believed that the Kansas-Nebraska Act represented but the opening maneuver of a sustained offensive by the planter class. While they engaged in no documented conspiracy and often found themselves deeply divided on specific issues, slaveholding politicians clearly did have common interests and ends to serve. Moreover, like all politicians, they caucused in private, thus giving the appearance of deeper conspiracy. It was also clear that many slaveholders sought room for the peculiar institution to expand, whether westward on the plains or southward into the Caribbean basin. As a result, 1854 witnessed besides the Kansas-Nebraska Act a major effort by some Southern politicians to make foreign policy serve the ends of slavery. The seizure by Havana officials of an American merchant vessel, the *Black Warrior*, brought from planters demands for war and Cuban annexation. William Marcy, Pierre

Soulé, John Mason, and James Buchanan, all diplomats subservient to Southern interests, moved to purchase Cuba from Spain.

At the same time, Southern extremists, or "fire-eaters," who entertained dreams of a sprawling Central American "slaveocracy" began agitating that the African slave trade, outlawed since 1808, be opened once again. Resumption would drive down slave prices, thus giving more poor whites the opportunity to enjoy the role of master. When William Walker, a Southerner, temporarily gained control of Nicaragua in 1855 by a coup d'etat and revoked that nation's emancipation decrees, antislavery Northerners felt even more fully confirmed in their grim determination to arrest the momentum of the "great slave-power conspiracy."

Many who needed still further confirmation of the "slave-power conspiracy" soon received it. Following the election of 1856, which saw the Republican Party's first presidential nominee, John C. Frémont, carry eleven Northern states while losing to Democrat James Buchanan, the United States Supreme Court announced its decision in the case of *Dred Scott vs. Sandford.* Scott, a slave, had been taken by his owner into territory declared free by terms of the Missouri Compromise. Aided by Gamaliel Bailey and seventy-five Northern congressmen, Scott had sued for his freedom. Speaking for a divided court, Chief Justice Roger B. Taney not only denied Scott's suit, but in a set of sweeping pronouncements gave slaveowning a theoretical standing in law which pleased even the most extreme planters. The Missouri Compromise, he declared, was unconstitutional; Congress possessed no power to legislate the limits of slavery's expansion. In another passage Taney added the gratuitous opinion that according to the Founding Fathers, blacks possessed no rights before the law that whites were "bound to respect." Slavery, in short, had been elevated to the status of a national institution. White supremacy had been enshrined as law. Horace Greeley, reform-minded editor of the New York *Tribune*, captured the essence of the resentments that more and more Northerners were coming to share as these proslavery events followed one another in ominous succession after 1854. "Slavery," he observed, "never left the North alone nor thought of so doing":

> "Buy Louisiana for us" said the slaveholders. "With pleasure." "Now Florida!" "Certainly." Next: "Violate your treaties with the Creeks and Cherokees; expel those tribes . . . so as to let us expand our plantations." "So said, so done." "Now for Texas!" "You have it." "Next a third of Mexico!" "Yours it is." "Now break the Missouri Compact and let slavery wrestle free labor for that vast region, consecrated by that Compact to Freedom!" "Very good. What next?" "Buy us Cuba!" "We have tried, but Spain refuses to sell it." "Then wrest it from her at all hazards!"

To this list anxious Northerners now added the Dred Scott decision.

How many more demands would they be forced to satisfy, opponents of slavery wondered, before this Southern colossus commanded the nation's destiny? What was to become of their vision of America as the "free society," a nation with a countryside peopled by independent, pious, and sober farmers? What other course was there but to ignore the Dred Scott decision and insist sternly that slavery's expansion be halted, here and now and forever— that the Wilmot Proviso be proclaimed the eternal law of the land? All over the North, these were the sentiments that politicians encountered from their constituents and that many of them now believed. So convinced, they abandoned their original parties en masse.

As abolitionists contemplated these crises, they began to remember older tactics and experience feelings of hesitation. Gerrit Smith, for instance, despite his fascination with violence, recoiled at the prospect of sectional collision. By 1857 he had embarked upon a quixotic crusade, accompanied by the famous pacifist Elihu Burritt, to promote compensated emancipation. Those same years also witnessed a resurgence of revivalism and evangelical abolitionism, especially in the rapid expansion of Lewis Tappan's American Missionary Association, which assisted blacks from Jamaica to Canada. As early as 1852 the A.M.A. maintained abroad five missions, thirteen stations, and sixteen physicians.

At the same time, many long-standing abolitionists tried to continue their time-honored political tactics. Garrisonians' arraignments of the Republican Party for its racism, conservatism, and temporizing policies remained unceasing during the later 1850's; "No Union with Slaveholders" remained their principal cry. Yet Wendell Phillips kept up his close private associations with Massachusetts Republicans like Charles Sumner and predicted the abolition of slavery "long before the nation has been converted into saints." Garrison likewise judged the rise of republicanism "the beginning of the end." Veterans like Gerrit Smith, Beriah Green, William Goodell, the Tappans, and Samuel J. May also engaged in the tactics of an earlier day, keeping their Liberty League alive as a separate abolitionist party dedicated to immediatism and federally legislated emancipation. In 1856 and 1860, Smith stood as the party's presidential nominee, attracting the support of some prominent black leaders like Frederick Douglass, Jermain Loguen, and James McCune Smith. Neither group developed much direct support, but both incessantly reminded voters that sectionalism ought to reflect higher ideals than a devotion to what Elizur Wright, Jr., called sarcastically "the white man's uncivil liberties."

In the end nearly all abolitionists outside Garrison's immediate coterie voted for the Republicans. They had fewer reservations about the party after Giddings, Chase, Seward, Wade, and other highly influential men began battling other more conservative elements which were attempting to make anti-Catholicism and immigrant restriction the focus of Republican concern. Among old-line Whigs especially, the issue of legislating against foreigners and Catholics seemed to offer the basis for organizing a new Unionist party which would silence forever all discord over slavery. By 1855, a splinter political party calling itself the Know-Nothings had taken form, based on an overtly anti-Catholic, anti-foreign platform.

Most abolitionists, like most evangelical Protestants, also harbored deep suspicions of the international Catholic hierarchy, the religion's formalistic liturgy, and the solid antiabolitionism of the Irish immigrants. Yet they agreed with the Republican opponents of nativism that discrimination against Catholics or foreigners would constitute a fundamental violation of the free-labor individualism which lay at the heart of the party's ideology. Moreover, to interject into American politics such "new and unconscionable elements of oppression," as Giddings once called them, would deflect attention from slavery, which was the "one real issue between the Republican party and those factions who stand opposed to it." Abolitionist hesitancy about supporting the emerging antislavery consensus thus decreased as the Know-Nothings' popularity declined in late 1855. Always erratic, but ever a bellwether of the abolitionists' feelings, Gerrit Smith (while running for president himself) contributed five hundred dollars to the 1856 presidential campaign of John C. Frémont.

Smith's actions symbolized the deep perplexities which were surfacing within abolitionism during the last years of the 1850's. While increasing numbers of immediatists tolerated antislavery conservatism by supporting the Republican Party, many simultaneously yearned for revolution. Ever since the late 1830's, abolitionists had been broadly divided between "reformers" and "radicals." But by 1858–1859, such designations had become meaningless. Now abolitionists seemed confronted by a most intolerable choice. They could submerge themselves in the wave of Republican antislavery, or they could applaud violent revolution. Most ended up attempting to do both, thanks primarily to John Brown and Abraham Lincoln. These two men by 1861 had largely satisfied the abolitionists' contrary impulses to avail themselves of both ballots and bullets.

Many abolitionists were actually less surprised than they admitted in October 1859 upon hearing that Brown and his armed band had been foiled while raiding Harpers Ferry, Virginia, hoping to provoke mutiny among the slaves. Indeed, some of abolitionism's most violence-prone figures —Samuel Howe, Thomas Wentworth Higginson, Gerrit Smith, Theodore Parker, Franklin L. Sanborn, George Luther Stearns, and Frederick Douglass—had helped to finance Brown's attack. Others had known generally that Brown was contemplating a violent course, and Brown himself often spoke openly about his plans. Blacks in Canada, such as Harriet Tubman and Jermain Loguen, as well as American leaders like Douglass were well informed by Brown himself of what was to transpire.

Besides, there were politicians and reformers by the score—among them Joshua Giddings, Wendell Phillips, William Goodell, Henry Wilson, Charles Francis Adams, Benjamin Wade, and George W. Julian—who had approved when Brown had pleaded at meetings for money to support his Kansas adventures. Brown's magnetism, his skill at manipulating others, his prophetic incandescence, had overwhelmed all these presumably responsible individuals. He satisfied their romantic desires to flirt with conspiracy. Openly or unconsciously, they yearned for a dramatic example of direct action, and Brown set off for Virginia. After many weeks of preparation, he and his desperate band of eighteen descended on Harpers Ferry, seized the federal arsenal, and took several hostages as they sought to incite insurrection among slaves and free blacks. But the startled slaves refused to join Brown's army of liberation, and soon his brigade had been routed by troops under Colonel Robert E. Lee's command. As his most recent biographers, Richard O. Boyer and Stephen Oates, demonstrate with such brilliance, "old Brown," an unimaginably complex man, was endowed with a personality of immense power. Yet perhaps the raid on Harpers Ferry can be best understood, not as Brown's supreme act of will, but as a predictable product of the abolitionists' half-articulated desire for confrontation which had been increasing in the antislavery movement ever since 1850.

It was little wonder then that so many rushed to embrace Brown's deeds as he was arraigned, given a semblance of a trial, then sentenced and finally hung by Virginia authorities in the winter of 1859. Brown orchestrated his own martyrdom with consummate skill, issuing statements to the press and composing letters which were quickly published. Meanwhile, New England's illuminati, Ralph Waldo Emerson, Henry Wadsworth Longfellow, and Henry David Thoreau, delivered eloquent paeans to Brown's courage and moral inspiration. In Brooklyn, Wendell Phillips electrified an immense audience, announcing that "the lesson of the hour is insurrection." Brown, Phillips declared, "has twice as much right to hang Governor Wise [of Virginia] as Governor

Wise has to hang him," for Brown had acted on the highest dictates of Christian duty. Lydia Maria Child, in turn, tried vainly to reconcile her nonresistance with her admiration for Brown by offering to nurse the old man in prison as he recovered from his wounds.

Some abolitionists, Garrison included, hurried to separate their belief in the slaves' inherent right to rebel from their genuine abhorrence of Brown's terrorism. Still others organized Christian antislavery conventions which tried to reassert the primacy of moral suasion. One of these, held in Chicago five days after the Harpers Ferry raid, was interrupted by black abolitionists who offered impassioned defenses of the events at Harpers Ferry.

But the most anxious of all to disassociate themselves from John Brown were the moderate and conservative leaders of the Republican Party, Abraham Lincoln among them. Hoping to end any confusion between themselves and "rank abolitionism," these Republicans took prominent roles in organizing the anti-Brown protest meetings that assembled in major cities. For his part, Lincoln attempted to explain Brown to the slaveholders as an aberration which appeared from time to time in world history, the lone, mad assassin. Brown, according to Lincoln, was simply the most recent of a long succession of randomly violent "enthusiasts," whose misguided deeds led each to "little else than his own execution."

Lincoln's explanation sounded astute on first hearing, but it was fundamentally inaccurate and wholly unconvincing to a violently outraged planter class. Even within Lincoln's own party, men like Benjamin Wade went so far as to blame the "slave power" for the Harpers Ferry raid by claiming that Brown had been driven to seek revenge for the "oppression" his family had suffered during the Kansas border wars. Charles Sumner, though far less disposed than

Wade to excuse Brown's acts, expressed his admiration for "many things in the *man.*" Most other sectionally militant Republicans did likewise. In the face of such statements, Lincoln's reassurances to the slaveholders were unconvincing. Republican efforts at moderation notwithstanding, it was now harder than ever for planters to distinguish a Salmon P. Chase from a Wendell Phillips, or even a Frederick Douglass from an Abraham Lincoln. The slaveholders' cries against the "nigger abolitionism of the black Republicans," which increased to a shrill pitch as the 1860 elections drew near, were thus quite understandable. They also contained important elements of truth.

For all its unabashedly racist supporters, for all of its platform promises not to meddle with slavery where it existed, for all its deafening official silence in 1860 on questions like the interstate and District of Columbia slave trades, the Republican Party also incorporated a crucial measure of biracial idealism. It did so first through the participation of the Wade brothers (Benjamin and Edward), Chase, Sumner, Giddings, John P. Hale, and George W. Julian, who had all avowed their fervent desire to hasten the end of slavery. The political upheavals of the 1850's, moreover, had added to this group such new men as Thaddeus Stevens, Owen Lovejoy (Elijah's brother), Charles Durkee, and Zachariah Chandler. If ever installed as the dominant party, the Republicans would certainly be pressed by such men to take direct measures against the planter class. Besides, the party also pledged in its 1860 presidential platform to support internal improvements, a Pacific railroad, a homestead law, and a tariff. Here were promises which, if implemented, would greatly augment federal power over regionalism in the nation's economic life. Clearly, ex-Democrats as well as ex-Whigs within the Republican Party had together decided by 1860 that "free soil, free labor, and free men" could not be ensured unless national authority reigned over the states' rights claims which had heretofore shielded slavery.

Wendell Phillips, who ceaselessly excoriated the Republicans for their conservatism, nevertheless appreciated these facts. In 1860, on the eve of Republican victory, he declared: "I value the success of the Republican party; not so much as an instrument, but as a milestone. It shows how far we [abolitionists] have got." For the same reasons, the Colored Man's National Suffrage Convention overwhelmingly endorsed the party, although some blacks like Henry Highland Garnet, repelled by the Republicans' racist elements, voted for Gerrit Smith instead of Abraham Lincoln.

Unlike Phillips, the planter class perceived the Republican Party as a direct instrument of abolitionism, and they did so for several good reasons. As the voting returns confirmed Lincoln's victory in 1860, slaveholders imagined what life would be like once they had begun to feel the effects of Republican executive power. No matter how often he reaffirmed his deep reservations about black equality and his abhorrence of abolitionism, it was indisputably clear that Lincoln regarded slavery as a moral perversion. Because of slavery, he once stated, "our republican robe is soiled, and trailed in the dust"; the institution, he declared, put the lie to all other American claims of republican liberty. Given such views, Lincoln would certainly veto any legislation which provided for the further expansion of slavery, despite the Dred Scott decision. In neither branch of Congress would proslavery strength be sufficient to override him. Meanwhile, Lincoln would certainly employ his immense patronage to appoint "black" Republicans to federal offices throughout the slave states. The prospect of Owen Lovejoy running the customs service in Charleston, South Carolina, or of Charles Francis Adams administering the post offices in Mississippi was beyond tolerating. With Lincoln in the White House, the planters feared, the American Anti-Slavery Society and its scheming British partners would at last enjoy free access to the plantation. Denied the expansion so necessary for survival, scorned by world opinion, and subverted from within, Southern civilization would then face extinction. Secession, indeed, provided the only possible escape, and the planters seized the chance.

To the relief of all abolitionists, Lincoln rejected any further compromise with Southern demands for the unlimited expansion of slavery. Sworn to uphold the Union by force of arms, he called for seventy-five thousand volunteers after South Carolinian troops had fired on the federal arsenal at Fort Sumter. By April 1861, whatever nonresistance, disunionism, and "antipolitics" were left within abolitionism vanished almost entirely as nearly everyone in the movement accepted the realities of civil war. Garrisonians and Liberty Leaguers together quoted John Quincy Adams, who once said that the circumstances of treasonous insurrection would endow Congress and the President with the power of emancipation. As the troops began to march, most abolitionists were discarding the last vestige of their romantic radicalism for the hard world of power politics. Simultaneously, they turned to their last, most awesome, most significant task of all. Somehow, they had to transform a civil war between two antagonistic civilizations into a revolution in race relations.

8

Triumph and Tragedy:
Abolitionists and Emancipation

During the last months of the Civil War, reporter Whitelaw Reid found himself in northern Alabama as he followed the Union Army. Looking for a story, he struck up a conversation with an emancipated slave who had taken shelter in an abandoned tent near the small town of Selma. What did this fellow expect, Reid wondered aloud, now that he was rid of his master? The black man answered easily and with emphasis: "I's want to be a free man, cum when I please, and nobody say nuffin' to me or order me aroun'." Long before Union armies invaded Alabama, abolitionists had begun demanding much the same things. Slavery must be destroyed and black Southerners guaranteed freedom, they had insisted. Only on these grounds of social justice could the carnage of warfare be justified and the "slave power" permanently defeated while the North purged itself of its disgraceful proslavery heritage.

Ultimately, the abolitionists were to witness a South which partially fulfilled yet cruelly blighted this black Alabamian's hopes for freedom and dignity. In the end, no person living in the United States would be able legally to claim another as chattel. In theory and, for a time, in practice, emancipated slaves were to enjoy full legal protection and civil rights, protected by Federal power, Constitutional amendments, and congressional acts. Abolitionists and agencies of government were to find themselves cooperating to provide some economic security to these new black citizens. But in the end, white reformers and former slaves would discover that the path of emancipation led to sharecropping, segregation, and the terrors of white vigilantism. The black Alabamian's descendants were not destined to come and go as they pleased, escape white coercion, and avoid being ordered around. The South's traditions of caste oppression, aristocracy, and rural parochialism, modified and intensified by military defeat, were finally to persist.

Yet as the Civil War revealed its brutal dimensions, in late 1861, abolitionists everywhere concerned themselves with a much more immediate matter, one closely connected with the fate of Southern society. Their task, quite simply, was to convince other Northerners that ending slavery, not preserving the Union, should be the overriding goal of the war. No Union, they argued, was worth preserving if it continued to uphold slavery. But as the first months after the firing on Fort Sumter passed, it became clear that most Republicans construed the war's meaning in any but abolitionist terms. Immediately following the rout of the Union Army at the first battle of Bull Run in August 1861, Congress declared that the sole purpose of this war was "to preserve the Union, with all the dignity, equality and rights of the several states unimpaired." In the House, Thaddeus Stevens, Owen Lovejoy, and other radical Republicans offered no remonstrance as this measure passed with only two dissenting votes. The *Springfield Republican* in Illinois, widely respected as a sounding board for Lincoln's own views, expressed the mood perfectly in June 1861, observing: "If there is one point of honor upon which . . . this administration will stick, it is its pledge not to interfere with slavery in the states."

A number of facts explain the Republicans' stance, which was in obvious conflict with the abiding hatred of slavery that the party's more radical members nurtured. For one thing, Lincoln and other leaders shared a deep preoccupation with retaining the loyalty of Unionist elements in Kentucky, northern Virginia, Tennessee, Maryland, Delaware, Missouri, and other border states. Of obvious military value, these areas had all known slavery. The whites in them were sensitive to states' rights and felt little good-will toward free blacks and abolitionists. Republicans feared that precipitous action against slavery would certainly risk driving these important states away from the Union cause.

Besides, radicals like Thaddeus Stevens were acutely aware that their party had captured a Northern majority precisely because it had stressed antislavery moderation. A very large bloc of race-conscious voters, especially in the Midwest, had endorsed free soil with enthusiasm, knowing that Abraham Lincoln was in no way pledged to destroy slavery in the South, either immediately or in some distant future. The 1860 Republican platform had disclaimed all such intention, and especially during the war's early phases, the Republican coalition was enormously complex and fragile. Clearly, the party would not be kept together by trumpet calls for emancipation. Throughout the war, even as Lincoln turned his policies toward abolition, he was constantly forced to reassure the party's conservative wing: "What I do about slavery and the colored race," he averred in 1862, "I do because it helps to save the Union; and what I forbear, I forbear because I do *not* believe it would help to save the Union."

But to abolitionists, statements like Lincoln's carried the

familiar ring of expediency which they had long ago come to expect from politicians. Especially in war time, Northern politics continued to value consensus over the reformers' moral imperatives. For this reason, abolitionists found themselves continuing to play some of their familar roles as moral critics. Meetings of the American Anti-Slavery Society continued as usual, as did the state and local gatherings. At these affairs, speakers of national prominence like William Lloyd Garrison, Frederick Douglass, Gerrit Smith, and Wendell Phillips rose to demand emancipation and to denounce the administration. Lincoln's decision in September 1861 to revoke General John C. Frémont's declaration of martial law which had freed every slave belonging to rebels in Missouri initiated open conflict between the Republican administration and the immediatists. Garrison, hearing of the President's action, declared that even if Lincoln was "six feet four inches high," he was "a dwarf in mind." Throughout the war, many abolitionists retained some of their alienation from government. Moral suasion remained their principal vehicle as they attempted, as always, to transform American attitudes toward slavery and race.

Yet there was no mistaking the enormous changes brought on by the war. Most obvious was that, for all his caution about antislavery, Abraham Lincoln was the furthest thing imaginable from Franklin Pierce. Similarly, the Republican Party was in no respect the equivalent of those proslavery organizations which had dominated antebellum politics. Instead, Republicans and their President presented the abolitionists with a perplexing mixture of conservatism and promise. A devotee of emigrationism, Lincoln had once offered a bill in Congress to abolish slavery in the District of Columbia which was so generous to masters and so unmindful of the slaves as to evoke widespread abolitionist wrath. His courtroom defense of a master seeking the return of a fugitive had earned him Wendell Phillips's famous sobriquet, "Slave-Hound from Illinois."

But at the same time, abolitionists approved of the Lincoln who had denied in 1858 that the Union could continue "half-slave, half-free." Plainly, Lincoln believed as he said so often before the war that this "slave power" rested upon the even more "monstrous injustice" of enslavement itself. Moreover, Frederick Douglass, one of Lincoln's bitterest critics, always "remained impressed with his entire freedom from popular prejudice against the black race." Like his party, Lincoln thus exemplified idealism as well as expedience, egalitarianism as well as racism. For all their efforts to remain uncompromised agitators, most abolitionists found themselves drawn toward Republicanism, supporting the party's candidates and applauding its consistently radical wing.

There were, to be sure, exceptions. A few nonresistants like Lydia Maria Child and Adin Ballou decried the war-making Republicans for "doing evil that good may come" and refused to support the party. In 1862 other old-time zealots such as Stephen S. Foster, Parker Pillsbury, and Aaron Powell declared Lincoln to be "as truly a slaveholder as Jefferson Davis" because of his hesitancy to endorse unequivocal emancipation. Yet most abolitionists approved of Garrison's support for the war, for "the Union without slavery," and for the Republican Party. By 1865, with the ending of hostilities, only Wendell Phillips and a small handful of followers still attempted to practice the art of "antipolitical politics."

Changes in circumstances also diminished the abolitionists' genuinely radical roles. Not the least of these was their sudden popularity. As their cause gained support throughout the North, many people no longer perceived abolition-

ists as wild extremists, and their growing prestige as folk
heroes diminished their capacity to confront conventional
values. Wendell Phillips, George B. Cheever, Gerrit Smith,
and William Goodell headed an impressive list of abolitionists who accepted invitations to speak in the nation's capital.
Phillips's visit and private interview with Lincoln prompted
the New York *Tribune's* Washington correspondent to
observe that "a year ago [he] would have been sacrificed to
the Devil of Slavery anywhere on Pennsylvania Avenue."
Now "he was introduced by Mr. Sumner on the floor of the
Senate. . . . The attentions of the Senator to the apostle of
Abolition were of the most flattering character."

Phillips, who defined himself wholly by his radical
commitments, thus found himself being domesticated. He
resisted and to some extent succeeded in preserving his
position. Most other abolitionists were far less successful.
Usually they put aside disagreements over reform versus
revolution, moral suasion versus political action, and violence versus nonresistance. "Events have so changed the
position of affairs that their old-time policies are no longer
applicable," reported a former Garrisonian in late 1861. But
with the ending of disputation also came a loss of that fine
ideological focus which had informed the original abolitionist temperament. Radical blacks, for example, abandoned
their revolutionary emigrationism entirely. Abolitionists still
espoused race equality and thus remained outside the
boundaries recognized by society; yet an elusive but
unmistakable agitational quality was fading from their
words and deeds even during the early 1860's.

For the most part, however, abolitionists tried to ensure
that those who adopted emancipation did so out of moral
conviction. Exploiting their new-found fashionability, they
once again called on the 1830's techniques of moral suasion
by publishing newspapers, organizing rallies, and stimulat-

ing petition campaigns. In May of 1862, for example, Sidney Howard Gay, for years the zealous Garrisonian press chief of the *National Anti-Slavery Standard*, became managing editor of Horace Greeley's august *New York Tribune*. In that same year, the *New York Independent*, underwritten by Lewis Tappan, was entrusted to the brilliant editorial care of fervent abolitionist Theodore Tilden who, with coeditor Henry Ward Beecher, turned the paper into a powerful emancipationist organ. As in the antebellum era, when political abolitionists cooperated with the Free-Soilers, these editors applauded the various antislavery measures which Republicans enacted during 1862. During this year, Congress approved and Lincoln signed measures for compensated emancipation in the District of Columbia, passed the Wilmot Proviso, and took steps to suppress the African slave trade.

Meanwhile, Garrison and Gerrit Smith tried to make their old technique of holding rallies and conventions fit the new cause of military emancipation. Together with Phillips, Edmund Quincy, Samuel Gridley Howe, George Stearns, and other radical Republicans, they organized Emancipation Leagues to oversee a major propaganda effort against conservative war aims. The League's Washington Chapter kept that city agitated by sponsoring a series of abolitionist speakers at the Smithsonian Institution. Lincoln was noticed in the audience more than once. The Massachusetts League, directed by a charter member of the American Anti-Slavery Society, Samuel Sewall, published nearly one hundred thousand emancipationist pamphlets in 1862 alone. The Leagues also undertook a large-scale petition campaign reminiscent of those in the 1830's. By mid-1862, petitions bearing thousands of signatures were flooding Washington. Through such activities, as James M. McPherson has shown,

abolitionists made up the vanguard of the drive for emancipation.

But for all this strenuous activity, the white abolitionists
were not primarily responsible for originating the mounting
tide of emancipationist feeling. They capitalized on it,
organized it, and channeled it into politics, but they did not
create it through moral suasion. Instead, it was the generals
and armies, together with the black people in the North and
South, who turned emancipation from an abstraction into
an imperative. Union military reverses, for one thing,
stimulated support for emancipation. While Union generals
like George B. McClellan and Irvin McDowell revealed
either their ineptitude or their preoccupation with political
maneuvering, they suffered major military losses, or skir-
mished to no apparent purpose with the Confederate forces.
As 1862 wore on, it became obvious to most Republicans
that this was to be a savage, protracted conflict. The "slave
power" was proving even more formidable in war than it
had in politics.

As a consequence, many Northerners began to suspect
that abolitionists and radical Republicans were speaking
with wisdom when they warned that the fundamental issues
raised by the war could never be resolved by the mere
restoration of the Union. It became increasingly clear, even
to those who felt deep antipathy to blacks, that to readmit
the planter aristocracy into the councils of the Republic
would be to reawaken the fundamental conflicts over slave
expansion, secession, nullification, civil liberties, violence,
homestead laws, banks, tariffs, and internal improvements
which had for so long divided the nation. Increasingly,
Northerners came to agree that political necessity dictated
emancipation. But to most, the question of how the freed
slaves were to be treated was of little importance. The logic

of politics and war was proving far more effective than moral suasion in making converts to abolitionism.

Even more influential were the activities of black people on both sides of the battle lines. In the North, blacks first agitated to be allowed to enlist in the army; once accepted, they fought with great distinction, even though they were paid significantly less until the last months of the war and were heavily discriminated against by their white commanders. Viewing military participation as the most practical abolitionism of all, Frederick Douglass issued the pamphlet *Men of Color, To Arms!*, which exhorted potential black soldiers with the thought that "liberty won by white men would lack half its lustre. [They] who would free themselves must strike the blow . . . Action! action! not criticism is the plain duty of this hour." By mid-1863, black troops were enlisting in regiments in Massachusetts, Ohio, Pennsylvania, and New York, and white abolitionists, especially Phillips, George Stearns, and Thomas Wentworth Higginson, played recruiting roles in these military organizations. But the Northern black soldiers, not their white sympathizers, were the ones who furnished the more eloquent testimony to the justice of ending slavery.

In the end it was, not free blacks or white abolitionists, but slaves in the South whose actions most hastened emancipation. Many slaves found themselves involved directly in the Confederate war effort, building bridges, digging trenches, excavating breastworks, and hauling supplies. Abolitionists and radical Republicans took note of these labors and argued that, since slavery was now employed by the Southern war machine, abolition constituted a military necessity. Other bondsmen chose a course of action which was of greater influence still upon Northern opinion. As Union armies occupied coastal areas of the Deep South and maneuvered in the border states, slaves by the thousands deserted their masters and sought the protection of federal authorities. Many thousands more suddenly discovered that their masters had fled, and they, too, placed themselves under the Union flag. By so doing, they presented federal authorities with a nagging set of problems intimately related to emancipation.

These black escapees could not be regarded as free citizens. Until mid-1862 even the Confiscation Acts passed by Congress allowing the seizure of rebel property were ambiguous regarding the disposition of slaves. Besides, what standing did such persons enjoy before civil magistrates and in the eyes of criminal law? Could their masters rightfully reclaim their chattel? Should federal authorities return escapees to the enemy? Or should the escapees be considered spoils of war, the bondsmen of Unionists instead of the bondsmen of slaveholders? Or were they really men and women who deserved legal protection and civil rights? Simply put, these refugees from slavery forced Northerners to ponder the meaning of emancipation in the most direct and practical terms.

But no matter what conclusions federal officials reached, their subsequent policies regarding the escapees generated support for emancipation. Democratic General George B. McClellan, no antislavery man, decided during 1861 and 1862 to return slaves to the enemy under a flag of truce. Lincoln, as noted, also initially opposed the idea of employing military means to commandeer the slaves of rebel planters and had overridden General Frémont's attempts to do so in Missouri. Lincoln's policy, like McClellan's, only heightened the demand for emancipation by provoking the charge that even the President and his generals were themselves falling victims to the "slave-power conspiracy."

In contrast to McClellan, Generals Benjamin F. Butler, Nathaniel Banks, and Rufus Saxon at various times designated black refugees in the coastal areas of Virginia and the Deep South as "contraband of war," a vague status intermediate between slavery and citizenship. Such a designation eventually permitted these Union generals to conscript thousands of ex-slaves into their armies as full soldiers and as noncombatants. Higginson, who took command of a "contraband" army in the South Carolina Sea Islands district in 1862, understood clearly the significance of this new policy, calling it "the most important fact in the solution of this whole Negro question." There was, indeed, merit in this assessment. Lincoln's own opinions on the black man's fighting skill rapidly changed. At first he felt that using blacks as combatants would "produce more evil than good," but by January 1, 1863, he had publicly reversed his position. His Emancipation Proclamation, issued on that date, called for recruiting "contrabands" into the army as freedmen, and black regiments were often more effective on the battlefield than their white counterparts. As "contrabands" and Northern free blacks dueled the "slave power" with muskets and pikes, Northerners found the continued denials of emancipation increasingly difficult to accept. The destruction of slavery was thus begun on the battlefield and then ratified in the Emancipation Proclamation. In this quite restricted but important sense, abolition was first achieved neither by Republican politicians nor by white abolitionists, but by those blacks, free and slave, who intruded into a white nation's civil war.

In late September 1862, Lincoln announced that the Republican Party was transforming the "War for Union" into a war to exterminate slavery. His preliminary Emancipation Proclamation was open to criticisms as being far too limited and too tainted with expedience. Lincoln hoped that his Proclamation would foster division among Confederates, stimulating "reunion" movements in the upper South and panic in the "cotton kingdom." Foreign powers, he further expected, might feel less inclined to aid the Confederacy if the North was pledged to the holy cause of obliterating slavery. Critics pointed out that the Proclamation abolished slavery only in the still-independent Confederacy where federal law exercised no practical power. In the Unionist border areas, slavery not only remained untouched, but was sustained by the 1850 Fugitive Slave Law until its repeal by Congress in mid-1864. Many abolitionists scanned the Proclamation and were distressed to find no mention of guarantees for the freedmen's civil rights, no provisions that would prevent emancipation from leading directly to a new era of less formal, but no less oppressive, servitude.

Stephen S. Foster, Parker Pillsbury, Wendell Phillips, and other radical abolitionists were not alone in deploring these weaknesses. Salmon P. Chase, now secretary of the treasury, complained to Joshua Giddings that the document did not formally guarantee that emancipation was to be permanent; freedmen, he feared, might still be subject to reenslavement in the future. Less radical Republicans entertained similar reservations. Lyman Trumbull, a moderate senator from Illinois, observed after reading the Proclamation that only a constitutional amendment could "insure that no state or Congress could ever restore slavery." Moreover, as abolitionists were fully aware, Lincoln had appended to this preliminary Proclamation a message in which he again proposed colonization and compensation. True, in the final Emancipation Proclamation of New Year's Day, 1863, the references to colonization were deleted. Yet Lincoln continued to emphasize that his Proclamation represented an act of necessity, not of morality, dictated by military and political considerations. "The President can do nothing for *freedom* in a direct manner, but only by circumlocution and delay," Garrison complained.

There was indeed something to be said for warnings like
Pillsbury's that the growing popularity of emancipation "as
'a military necessity'" represented a major threat to
long-established abolitionist doctrines. Lydia Maria Child
had exclaimed in early 1862 that "everything *must* go
wrong if there is no [change of] heart or conscience," if the
slaves were granted emancipation "merely as a 'war necessity.'" For over three decades abolitionists had struggled to
eradicate the biases of white society. They had expressed
active concern for the rights of free blacks and had long
made clear their belief that the slaves, once freed, should be
guaranteed legal protection and civil justice. But even as the
President proclaimed emancipation, it was clear that "moral
revolution" remained as distant as it had been in the 1830's.
Most who cheered Lincoln's Proclamations saw them as a
means to punish the arrogant slaveholding classes by
installing free-labor communities where plantations had
held sway and to cripple the war effort in the South. Here
were considerations markedly removed from the religious
imperatives which had, for so long, informed the white
reformers' movement for immediate emancipation.

Black abolitionists, however, generally acclaimed Lincoln's announcement. In spite of the Proclamation's weaknesses, most of their white colleagues joined them enthusias-
tically. On New Year's Day 1863, exponents of the "two
abolitionisms" mingled with ease, anxious to celebrate the
promulgation of slave emancipation. For all its shortcom-
ings, the practical-minded black abolitionists properly regarded the Emancipation Proclamation as an irrevocable
step toward racial freedom. Once the Proclamation was
announced, the chances that three million black people
would ever again be legally treated as property became
remote. From now on, the Union Army would march
through the rebellious states automatically emancipating

slaves as it went. Moreover, blacks could now reasonably expect to confront a new political order in America, no less racist, but one which no longer gave preponderance to a small group of powerful Southern exploiters. Perhaps these considerations were what prompted Douglass to exclaim in February 1863 that the Emancipation Proclamation constituted "the greatest event in our nation's history." Certainly Douglass was aware that the cheers which accompanied emancipation most often echoed hatred of slaveholders and not concern for the well-being of blacks. Yet the final disposition of the freedmen's future now seemed an open question, one perhaps susceptible to progressive solutions.

Fulfilling as emancipation was for white abolitionists, few saw their tasks ending during the war years. They sensed, as did many voters and politicians, that the major aims of both the war against the "slave power" and their own thirty-year crusade would never be fully achieved unless slavery was formally condemned in the Constitution. From January 1863 to December 1865, abolitionists campaigned vigorously with Republican groups for the enactment of the Thirteenth Amendment. Here, as in the thrust for emancipation itself, the abolitionists displayed energy and spoke with zeal as they again circulated petitions, joined lecture tours, and organized rallies. Yet these one-time extremists once more found themselves working well within the political system.

Even the most conservative Republicans now agreed that slavery must be expunged from the nation's laws. Indeed, they often assured their constituents that to abolish slavery was in no way to challenge the fact that America was preeminently a white man's country. White supremacy in the North, they emphasized, had not been subverted by emancipation during the 1790's. Why should anyone fear a contrary result in 1865? Yet for abolitionists there was now no suitable equivalent to the old Liberty Party or the now-anachronistic cry of "No Union with Slaveholders," no similar tool which abolitionists could employ to disrupt and edify the political process. Searching in vain for just such a device, Phillips, Pillsbury, Foster, Aaron Powell, and others finally broke with the main body of abolitionists and denounced Lincoln's presidency. Uniting with a small group of radical Republicans, they organized a dissident convention in Cleveland to nominate John C. Frémont in Lincoln's stead as the Republican standard-bearer in the elections of 1864. The result was not a serious reformulation of means and ends, but a round of bitter squabbles between Garrison and Phillips which soon preoccupied all of abolitionism's national leadership.

Through incidents such as these, ordinary political partisanship, scorned for so long by abolitionists as contrary to their exalted moral purpose, made permanent inroads within the American Anti-Slavery Society. Nearly every abolitionist supported Lincoln's reelection with enthusiasm in 1864 and praised the wisdom of his leadership when on April 9, 1865, Lee formally surrendered at Appomattox. The news of Lincoln's assassination five days later left veteran abolitionists no less shocked and genuinely bereaved than any other group of devoted Northerners. Then, on December 29, 1865, after the Thirteenth Amendment was finally ratified, Garrison declared the abolitionists' original mission to be fulfilled. As Phillips issued torrents of protest, Garrison terminated publication of the *Liberator* forever and announced that the antislavery societies no longer served any useful purpose. Instead, he advised, abolitionists should either work individually to assist blacks or join with the many recently established groups which now sponsored projects to aid the newly freed slaves. By 1866, Garrison, Phillips, and their lawyers were contesting in court to determine whether a cash bequest from an old abolitionist should be used for freedmen's aid or for subsidizing the publications of the American Anti-Slavery Society. As the South sued for peace and the Reconstruction era opened, the abolitionist movement was rapidly fragmenting, exhausting both its powers of agitation and its capabilities as a coherently radical enterprise.

While Phillips, Pillsbury, Foster, and their handful of followers tried throughout the 1860's to recapture their radical roles, most abolitionists made an easy, but significant peace with the new circumstances. For so long informed by the absolutes of romanticism, many reformers had now accommodated themselves to the pragmatic demands of step-by-step social amelioration. As George Fredrickson has shown, the rigors of war had already fostered among abolitionists a new sense of mundane practicality. After 1861 the pressures to mobilize, to enforce military discipline even on the "home front," had led many reformers away from unfettered individualism. Garrison, for all his years of perfectionist zeal, reflected this change of mood in 1865 by closing the *Liberator* and calling for freedmen's aid. Clearly, he saw himself not as retiring from reform, but as shifting the focus of his career to fit a new era. Long-standing Garrisonian J. Miller McKim, however, best captured the essence of abolitionism's last phase when he wrote that "iconoclasm has had its day" and that the "old antislavery routine" of agitating was now passé. "For the battering-ram we must substitute the hod and trowel," he advised, for "we have passed through the pulling down stage of our movement; the *building up* . . . remains to be accomplished." With slavery facing permanent extinction, many abolitionists now turned eagerly to the step-by-step task of aiding the South's black freedmen.

Even during the war, practical-minded abolitionists like

McKim had begun projects to aid the black Southerner's transition from slavery. In late 1861, Union forces seized the Sea Islands, including the town of Port Royal, off the South Carolina coast. The planters fled, leaving behind nearly ten thousand slaves and perhaps the richest alluvial lands in the nation for growing long staple cotton. For one last time, Lewis Tappan gathered together veteran abolitionists and New England philanthropists, who, with Salmon Chase in the Treasury Department, helped to underwrite benevolent groups. By mid-1862, doctors, teachers, labor superintendents, and supplies were streaming into the Sea Islands. As Willie Lee Rose has demonstrated, these "Gideonites," as the Port Royal abolitionists called themselves, soon succeeded in establishing schools in which the freedmen learned eagerly and easily. In the cotton fields, meantime, blacks worked with industry and innovation as wage-earning free laborers. For all of its tribulations with government bureaus and white paternalism, the "Port Royal Experiment" indicated from the first that recently enslaved black Southerners were fully able to maintain very productive free communities so long as they were provided with three things: political support, military protection, and material assistance.

Abolitionists, however, were only capable of furnishing the last of these three prerequisites. During Reconstruction, the power to provide political support and military protection resided almost exclusively with the Republican majority in Congress. Hence, the several thousand teachers, philanthropists, and political organizers who traveled South were acutely aware of the importance of decisions made by politicians in Washington. So were the many nationally famous abolitionist leaders like Garrison, Whittier, Smith, Phillips, Weld, Chapman, the Stantons, and Child, who were now administering Education Societies and Freedmen's Aid Commissions which solicited funds and recruits for Southern projects.

Early 1865 found many of these individuals, including a contingent of black abolitionists headed by George Downing, lobbying openly in Washington for the expansion of the Freedmen's Bureau, a federal agency created at the close of the war to assist the resettlement of emancipated slaves. Chartered by Congress in 1865 after three years of lobbying by abolitionists like Samuel G. Howe and McKim, the Freedmen's Bureau quickly became essential to Yankee efforts to remake Southern life. The Bureau's appropriations underwrote school construction, paid the moving expenses of Northern teachers, and supplied books and equipment.

By 1866, however, some abolitionists had concluded that such activities would not guarantee the freedmen's future. Wendell Phillips Garrison, son of "the original liberator," expressed feelings which now enjoyed support among the most radical abolitionists and Republicans. "To free the slave, and then abandon him in an anomalous position betwixt bondage and manhood" was as cruel an act as enslavement itself, he wrote. Calling instead for the complete reorganization of Southern society, he demanded that the federal government adopt a policy of "absolute justice." The reconstruction of the South must be "thorough," he emphasized, "and affect its constitutions, statutes and customs."

To abolitionists such a program now meant that the federal government should confiscate the vast tracts belonging to rebel planters and redistribute them in forty-acre allotments to the former slaves. Retributive justice as well as the dictates of philanthropy could be satisfied, they argued, only if the guiltless freedmen were compensated for the generations of exploitation they and their forebears had endured. Besides, as abolitionists like young Garrison were well aware, black freedom in the South would have permanence only if the ex-slaves controlled a significant share of the region's economic resources. Otherwise, blacks might enjoy the theoretical guarantees of equal legal protection and even vote in every election, yet still remain powerless before their vengeful white neighbors.

Their demands for the education of freedmen and black equality in civil rights thus culminated and terminated the abolitionists' crusade. Indeed, their attempts to revolution-ize race hierarchy and class position in the old slave states seemed in some ways to have brought them full circle, and were reminiscent of their efforts in the North before the war. "Gideonite" teachers instructing black children in the Carolina Sea Islands certainly harked back to Prudence Crandall's protracted struggles in the 1830's to open her girls' school to black children. Abolitionist memorials that Congress guarantee the freedmen's civil rights recalled the days when they had petitioned state legislators and filed suits to end disenfranchisement in the North. Their insist-ence on land redistribution and black economic uplift in the South had likewise been prefigured in Lewis Tappan's sponsorship of manual-labor academies for Northern blacks and in Gerrit Smith's abortive attempts to found black free-labor colonies on his estates. For decades, abolitionists of both races had sought by such means to demonstrate to racist disbelievers the capacity of oppressed black people to become full and productive citizens. Now, on a much expanded scale, the Port Royal experiment, the work of the Freedmen's Bureau, and the agitation for guarantees of black enfranchisement offered much the same prospect.

Wendell Phillips, however, accurately glimpsed even more profound continuities which linked the abolitionists' final efforts at Southern reconstruction to the turbulent antebellum decades. The Civil War, he insisted, was not just a struggle arising from disagreements over slavery, party platforms, and the nature of the Union. It was, to be sure, made up of all of these things, but it was also much more—an ultimate collision of two irreconcilable cultures. "What is the history of our seventy years?" he asked audiences on the eve of Union victory. "It is the history of two civilizations constantly struggling, and always at odds, *except when one or the other rules.*" The North, he explained, exemplified "the civilization of the nineteenth century" with its complete adherence to the "equal and recognized manhood" of "free labor, free speech, open Bibles, the welcome rule of the majority [and] the Declaration of Independence." The South, in entire antithesis, contained anachronisms which recalled "the days of Queen Mary and the Inquisition." It was an "aristocracy of the skin" intolerant of free inquiry, hostile to self-rule, wedded to "violence," blighted by "ignorance," mired in "idleness," and dedicated to the axiom "that one-third of the race is born booted and spurred, the other two-thirds ready for that third to ride." The war's deepest meaning, Phillips emphasized, could be understood only if seen as part of a much longer struggle for a common republican nationality in America. True peace therefore could be achieved, not by signing treaties or by enacting laws, but by "carrying Massachusetts to Carolina," by applying "Northern civilization all over the South." Every inherited privilege, every form of parochialism and patriarchy, must be uprooted from the Southern landscape. In their places a class of independent yeomen and artisans must arise, free laborers whose productive efforts supported common schools, free churches, and democratic institutions of all sorts. "We must take up the South and organize it anew," Phillips urged, "to absorb six millions of ignorant, embittered, bedeviled Southerners [black and white] and transmute them into honest, decent, educated Christian mechanics, worthy to be brothers of New England Yankees."

Expressed with the eloquence and redoubled force of finality, here once again was the vision which had shaped in some way every facet of the North's long crusade against slavery. As abolitionists hurried south, they spoke of "planting the Northern pine" in the Southern cotton fields. What they expressed by this phrase was their intention to follow Phillips's advice, to eradicate race inequality and provincial "ignorance" with the leveling codes of the Bible and the McGuffey reader. Long before, back in Boston in 1833, the original signers of the Declaration of Sentiments of the American Anti-Slavery Society had entertained identical hopes for a South of the future. Now, for a brief period in the mid-1860's, as they demanded ballots, land, education, and direct governmental protection for the freedmen, these abolitionists glimpsed the tantalizing, unattainable prospect of ultimate success.

Yet the initiative in shaping Reconstruction lay not with the abolitionists but with the Republican Congress. Here, for a time, reformers saw great cause for hope. Within the party's initially small but clearly abolitionist wing, senators and representatives such as Charles Sumner, Benjamin Wade, Thaddeus Stevens, George W. Julian, and Owen Lovejoy openly shared the old immediatists' desire to remake Southern society by supporting its black population. Yet by 1866 and 1867, the pro-Southern policies of Lincoln's successor, Andrew Johnson, together with the recalcitrance of the defeated Confederates, had driven a huge bloc of moderate and even conservative Republicans also to insist on a stringent Reconstruction program. Johnson's pardoning of prominent rebels, his approval of state-enacted "black codes" which were highly prejudicial to the freedmen, his veto of the bill extending the Freedmen's Bureau's life and, above all, his insistence that Reconstruction policy lay entirely within his presidential prerogative, made Republicans in Congress suddenly fear that they had won the war only to lose the peace. The "slave power," it seemed, remained as actively conspiratorial as ever, now invading the offices of the Chief Executive, contriving to reestablish slavery in all but name, and working toward the overthrow of the Republican Party. Once again, and for the last time, an antislavery consensus established itself in majority politics; idealism and political realism once again supported one another as Congress enacted legislation designed to ensure that ex-slaves would remain full citizens.

Of course, abolitionists' expectations of fulfillment through radical Reconstruction were ill-founded. For all the sincerity of the Sumners and Stevenses, Republican efforts to combat Andrew Johnson proved no more akin to a fundamental shift in racial attitudes than had most opposition to the "slave power" touched off back in 1854 by the Kansas-Nebraska Act. "Moral revolution" remained as elusive as ever. As rank-and-file Republican voters went to the polls in the later 1860's, for example, many of their representatives urged them to vote for the Fourteenth and Fifteenth Amendments which Congress had designed explicitly to uphold the rights of the freedmen. Such measures, they were told, would assure the freedman's contentment with his life and lessen the threat of a massive black exodus into the North. In many areas, especially in urban centers and in regions close to the South border states, racist opinion arrayed itself in vocal opposition to the Republican's Southern policies.

As a result, no matter how enlightened his private views on race might be, no Republican Party leader could avoid being influenced by racism in the electorate. Extensive land confiscations and redistribution to the freedmen likewise proved too sweeping a plan, considering the Republicans' broad commitment to upholding the right of private property. In late 1865, when Andrew Johnson returned to their original owners most of the lands already distributed to freedmen, only a few Republicans issued serious remonstrances. Many abolitionists likewise adopted a wary posture toward expanding the federal government's power in the South. Their own long-standing belief in the efficacy of individual initiative led many of them to oppose confiscation and to declare, early on, that the freedmen must "elevate themselves" by their own efforts. In other respects, too, radical Reconstruction was characterized not by severity, but by mildness and brevity. In several of the old Confederate states such as Virginia, the period of federally supported radical rule lasted less than a year. Border slave states, like Tennessee, experienced hardly any Reconstruction at all, and throughout the South the number of federal forces deployed to uphold black civil rights was usually minimal. Even the radical Republicans, once pictured as American "Jacobins," have been shown to have been far more moderate and willing to compromise than had once been supposed. Up to the very end of the era, into the late 1870's and 1880's, those abolitionists who remained at all vocal were still to find themselves protesting the majority's racial prejudices and the moral negligence of politicians.

Yet once the rebel states had complied with all the Republicans' congressional demands and had been readmitted to the Union, what could abolitionists do to further ensure the freedom of the South's black citizens? Some continued to lobby for legislation like the Civil Rights Act that Charles Sumner sponsored in the twilight of his career, in 1874 and 1875. Others tried to keep the Republican Party mindful of its antislavery principles and opposed the efforts of liberal Republicans in 1872 to lead the party to other issues. Meanwhile, abolitionist veterans took care to inculcate in their children the traditions of the movement, a fact which explains why so many of them were to be found decades later underwriting black universities in the South and supporting nascent civil rights groups in the North. Atlanta, Fisk, and Howard universities as well as Talladega, Spelman, and Tougaloo colleges were initially founded with abolitionist help. In the 1870's, moreover, a young W. E. B. Du Bois was discovering models for his own luminous career in Frederick Douglass, Martin Delany, and Wendell Phillips. Abolitionism's legacy for ensuing civil rights and black liberation struggles was reconfirmed even as the movement consigned itself to history.

Meanwhile, the Republican commitment to the black race, always tenuous, soon wavered and finally collapsed. The Wades and the Julians retired, were voted out of office, or went on to espouse other causes. In their place came "Gilded Age" politicians and civil service reformers, men who spoke for powerful constituencies which hardly perceived race reform as synonymous with national, sectional, or class interest. Following the elections of 1876, when the Southern states again assumed total control of their racial affairs, abolitionists protested strongly. Those citizens who nodded in agreement felt no compulsion to do anything; without constituents, abolitionism became only a series of noble utterances, not a compelling call to action.

Little wonder that many of those immediatists who still yearned for social change embraced other causes—Phillips adopted labor reform, women's rights, municipal reform, and a host of other movements. Lysander Spooner explored libertarian atheism, while Elizur Wright, Jr., revolutionized the life-insurance industry by inventing actuarial tables. Susan B. Anthony, Elizabeth Cady Stanton, and Lucretia Mott were only among the best-known abolitionists to lead the new postbellum drive for women's rights. Many of these same women and a number of male abolitionists took on the task of eliminating prostitution in the cities and "improving" the morals of the immigrant.

All the while, blacks in the South made their way in a new world, a world without slavery. True, it was a world peopled with hostile whites. Some were powerful planters who still commanded massive numbers of black laborers as sharecroppers. Other vengeful whites delighted in lynch mobs. Civil rights laws and access to the franchise often meant little, but sometimes they could signify much, as the blacks who participated in the Farmer's Alliances of the 1880's and Populist revolt of the 1890's were to demonstrate. Most important, however, in the new South there was no legal buying and selling of people, no constant, crippling threat of personal disruption which had so seriously constricted the slave's autonomy. Here, perhaps, was what the black refugee had meant as he told Whitelaw Reid of his wish to "be a free man, [and] cum when I please." In retrospect, the differences between formal enslavement and systematic exploitation as a sharecropper might seem small. In light of testimony taken during the 1930's from ex-slaves who survived both eras, however, such was hardly the case.

Abolitionists could not really claim that their thirty-year movement had led directly to the destruction of slavery, and most of them admitted that theirs had been, at best, an ambiguous victory. Generals Sherman and Grant, not Garrisonians and Liberty men; warfare between irreconcilable cultures, not moral suasion, had intervened between the master and his slave. Emancipation left America not clothed in righteousness, but reconfirmed in its white supremacism. Frederick Douglass took final stock of the era of emancipation this way: "Liberty came to the freedmen . . . not in mercy, but in wrath, not by moral choice, but by military necessity, not by the generous action of the people among whom they were to live, . . . but by strangers, foreigners, invaders, trespassers, aliens and enemies."

Abolitionists, in short, ultimately remained bound by the limits of their age. To continue with Douglass's words, "Nothing was to have been expected other than what has happened." But if the crusaders against slavery did not cause history to be shaped in a happier form, one more reassuring for us to read, they did attempt to explore the maximum possibilities for social justice in their own times. The ambiguous results of their efforts, the obvious failures and the tentative successes, all indicate the power of race, class, and ideologies to order and disrupt their society, and our own as well.

In our industrial age, where urban segregation has replaced the plantation as the primary means of white dominion, it hardly suffices to conclude simply that the abolitionists failed to master the era that had created them. Instead, we must continue to analyze their ideas and actions, to seek understanding of how they both reinforced and transformed the dominant features of pre-Civil War America. Clearly, abolitionists could neither dictate the outcome of events nor comprehend fully their own motives and responsibilities. Yet these holy warriors have left a profound imprint on our national memory, one impossible to eradicate. For this reason, the history of their movement will never cease to provoke and instruct people who demand an America based on justice among peoples of all races.

Bibliography

What follows makes no pretense to completeness. In this bibliography I hope only to make useful suggestions to undergraduates and to indicate some of the works which have most informed my own thoughts as I wrote this book.

Prologue: Slavery in Republican America

One good introduction to abolitionism is an analysis of the way historians have interpreted the movement during the past several decades. Since abolitionism has always been associated with controversial issues, it is not surprising that historians have been divided deeply in their opinions of the movement's significance and validity. Merton Dillon, "The Abolitionists, A Century of Historiography, 1959–1969," *Journal of Southern History* (December 1969), is a useful analysis of recent academic opinion on these questions. Richard O. Curry (ed.), *The Abolitionists, Reformers or Fanatics?* (1973), reprints a well-balanced selection of conflicting historical writings. There are also several general histories of abolitionism which introduce the movement. Best among them remains Louis Filler, *The Crusade Against Slavery, 1830–1860* (1960), along with Merton Dillon, *The Abolitionists: The Growth of a Dissenting Minority* (1973).

The abolitionists can introduce themselves through their own writings. In many libraries, microfilm copies of abolitionist newspapers are available. The memoirs of leading abolitionists have also been reprinted. Good anthologies of abolitionist writings which reproduce shorter pieces are also easy to obtain, including John L. Thomas, *Slavery Attacked* (1965); Louis Ruchames, *The Abolitionists* (1964); Truman Nelson, *Documents of Upheaval, Selections from the Liberator* (1966); Herbert Aptheker, *Documentary History of the Negro People*, Vol. I (1968); and most serviceable of all, W. H. Pease and Jane H. Pease, *The Antislavery Argument* (1965). Several collections of the letters of major abolitionists have also been published. Louis Ruchames and Walter Merrill are responsible for the *Letters of William Lloyd Garrison* (1971–   ), Dwight L. Dumond edited *The Letters of James Gillespie Birney, 1831–1857* (1938), and Dumond collaborated with Gilbert Hobbs Barnes in editing *The Letters of Theodore Dwight Weld, Angelina Grimké Weld and Sarah Grimké, 1822–1844* (1941). Philip Foner edited *The Life and Writings of Frederick Douglass* (1950–1955).

The abolitionists cannot be properly studied without attention to the institution that evoked their opposition. For the origins of American slavery and white racism, Winthrop Jordan, *White Over Black: American Attitudes toward the Negro, 1550–1812* (1968), is essential, while Peter Wood, *Black Majority: Negroes in South Carolina* (1975), is equally brilliant in analyzing the early evolution of black society. Eugene Genovese, *Roll Jordan Roll* (1975), explores many facets of black culture in the slave South and examines profoundly the master-slave relationship. This work, like Eugene Genovese, *Political Economy of Slavery* (1967), emphasizes the "precapitalist," hierarchical features of the Southern economy and social setting. Kenneth Stampp, *The Peculiar Institution* (1959), remains a valuable description of slavery, while Carl Bridenbaugh, *Myths and Realities of the Colonial South* (1959), is a wise introduction to that region. Slavery in the North is described in Edward McManus, *Black Bondage in the North* (1970).

Finally, there are several works which set abolitionism in broader patterns of historical development and academic controversy which responsible students should not neglect. Some of these include Barrington Moore, *The Social Origins of Dictatorship and Democracy* (1966), especially Chapter 3; C. Duncan Rice, *The Rise and Fall of Black Slavery* (1975); Stanley Elkins, *Slavery: A Problem in American Institutional and Intellectual Life* (1959), especially Part 4; Raimondo Luarghi, "The Civil War and the Modernization of American Society," *Civil War History* (September 1972); Eric Foner, "The Causes of the American Civil War: Recent Interpretations and New Directions," *Civil War History* (August

1974); Aileen Kraditor, "American Radical Historians on Their Heritage," *Past and Present* (August 1972); John S. Rosenberg, "Toward a New Civil War Revisionism," *American Scholar* (Spring 1969).

1. Abolitionism in Early America

Two works by David Brion Davis are essential to understanding abolitionism prior to the nineteenth century: *The Problem of Slavery in Western Culture* (1966), and *The Problem of Slavery in the Age of Revolution, 1770–1823* (1974). Davis's focus is international as he analyzes the complex interplay of evangelicalism, rationalism, and commercial capitalism in the rise of western antislavery. Thomas E. Drake, *Quakers and Slavery in America* (1950), is a useful survey, while Mary S. Locke, *Antislavery in America from the Introduction of African Slaves to the Prohibition of the Slave Trade, 1619–1808* (1901), supplies myriad facts, if little else. Winthrop Jordan, *White Over Black: American Attitudes toward the Negro, 1550–1812* (1968), and Duncan J. MacLeod, *Slavery, Race and the American Revolution* (1974), address the relationships between slavery and the American quest for independence.

The progress of Northern abolitionism in the Revolutionary era is analyzed well in Arthur Zilversmit, *The First Emancipation: The Abolition of Slavery in the North* (1967). Benjamin Quarles, *The Negro in the American Revolution* (1961), chronicles black efforts at self-emancipation. In Ira Berlin, *Slaves without Masters: The Free Negro in the Antebellum South* (1974), the limits of Southern antislavery are explored along with the fascinating history of free blacks in the South. Other works which bear on Southern slavery and antislavery during the Revolution include Robert McColley, *Slavery in Jeffersonian Virginia* (1964), and Edmund S. Morgan, *American Slavery and American Freedom* (1975). The relationships among slavery, antislavery, and the politics of the Republic after 1787 are explored in the following works: David Brion Davis, *The Problem of Slavery in the Age of Revolution, 1770–1823* (1974); Duncan J. MacLeod, *Slavery, Race, and the American Revolution* (1974); Donald Robinson, *Slavery in the Structure of American Politics, 1765–1820* (1971); and Staughton Lynd, *Class Conflict, Slavery and the United States Constitution* (1967).

Alice D. Adams, *The Neglected Period of American Antislavery, 1808–1831* (1908), is bereft of interpretation but stuffed with facts. Phillip J. Staudenraus, *The African Colonization Movement* (1961), supersedes earlier treatments, while George Fredrickson, *The Black Image in the White Mind: The Debate on Afro-American Character and Destiny, 1817–1914* (1971), puts colonization and many other antebellum white efforts to "solve the Negro problem" in a broad context of racist and reform thought. Specific slavery-related political crises of the early nineteenth century are treated in Glover Moore, *The Missouri Controversy, 1819–1821* (1953), and in William W. Freehling, *Prelude to Civil War: The Nullification Crisis in South Carolina, 1816–1836* (1966), a book with a much broader focus than the title might seem to imply. John Lofton chronicles the Denmark Vesey slave revolt in *Insurrection in South Carolina* (1964), but this work should be counterbalanced by Richard C. Wade, "The Vesey Plot Reconsidered," *Journal of Southern History* (April 1964).

2. The Commitment to Immediate Emancipation

To appreciate the relationships among evangelical religion, economic change, and the rise of abolitionism, one must confront at once Gilbert H. Barnes, *The Antislavery Impulse, 1830–1844* (1933), and Whitney Cross, *The Burnt-Over District: The Social and Intellectual History of Religious Enthusiasm in Western New York* (1950). Other especially valuable writings include John L. Thomas, "Romantic Reform in America, 1815–1865," *American Quarterly* (Summer 1965); William G. McLaughlin, "Pietism and the American Character," *American Quarterly* (Winter 1965); David Brion Davis, "The Emergence of Immediatism in British and American Antislavery Thought," *Mississippi Valley Historical Review* (September 1962); and Ann C. Loveland, "Evangelicalism and Immediate Emancipation in American Antislavery Thought," *Journal of Southern History* (May 1966). For an eloquent example of how evangelical religiosity could be transformed into black radicalism, see Charles M. Wiltse (ed.), *David Walker's Appeal* (1965).

Attempts to probe the deeper socio-psychological wellsprings of the abolitionist commitment have created a large and uneven literature. Unstinting sympathy with abolitionist goals leads to an excessive preoccupation with defending the reformers' "normality" in Martin Duberman, "The Abolitionists and Psychology," *Journal of Negro History* (July 1962), and Gerald Sorin, *The New York Abolitionists: A Case Study of Political Radicalism* (1971). David Donald, "Toward a Reconsideration of the Abolitionists," in *Lincoln Reconsidered* (1956), fails to locate properly the sources of abolitionism in changes in social status, a defect brilliantly remedied in Leonard Richards, *"Gentlemen of Property and Standing": Anti-Abolition Mobs in Jacksonian America* (1970). Yet it is hard to deny Donald's contention that many pious young people first found themselves deeply alienated from the world around them, a circumstance which helped to spur their commitments to abolitionism. Bertram Wyatt-Brown so argues in articles such as "Prelude to Abolitionism: Sabbatarian Politics and the Rise of the Second Party System," *Journal of American History* (September 1971), and "New Leftists and Abolitionists: A Comparison of American Radical Styles," *Wisconsin Magazine of History* (Summer 1970). Most recently, some historians have begun to explore the inner components of the abolitionists' publicly expressed ideology. See especially Ronald Walters, "The Erotic South: Civilization and Sexuality in American Abolitionism," *American Quarterly* (Summer 1973), and Lewis Perry, " 'We Have Had Conversation in the World': The Abolitionists and Spontaneity," *Canadian Journal of American Studies* (Spring 1975).

The form and ill-fate of the upper South antislavery movement can be followed in Merton Dillon, *Benjamin Lundy and the Struggle for Negro Freedom* (1966); Gordon E. Finnie, "The Antislavery Movement in the Upper South before 1840," *Journal of Southern History* (August 1969); and James Brewer Stewart, "Radicalism and the Evangelical Strain in Southern Antislavery Thought during the 1820's," *Journal of Southern History* (August 1974). William H. Freehling, *Prelude to Civil War* (1966), helps to illuminate the racial and political crises of the late 1820's and early 1830's, while Richard H. Brown, "The Missouri Crisis, Slavery, and the Politics of Jacksonianism," *South Atlantic Quarterly* (Winter 1966), explains the proslavery direction taken by mass politics during the 1820's. The effect of external crises on nascent abolitionism in the early 1830's receives attention in James Brewer Stewart, "Politics and Ideas in Abolitionism," *South Atlantic Quarterly* (December 1975). The following works illuminate various broader aspects of either romantic social thought or immediatist ideology: Donald G. Matthews, "The Abolitionists on Slavery: The Critique behind the Social Movement," *Journal of Southern History* (May 1967); Bertram Wyatt-Brown, "Stanley Elkins' *Slavery*: The Antislavery Interpretation Re-examined," *American Quarterly* (May 1973); and David Rothman, *The Discovery of the Asylum* (1970).

3. Mobs and Martyrs: The Dynamics of Moral Suasion

For the interplay of moral-suasion tactics, mob violence, the postal and petition campaigns, and the gag-rule struggles and their impact on abolitionism in the 1830's, see James Brewer Stewart, "Peaceful Hopes and Violent Experiences, the Evolution of Radical and Reforming Abolitionism, 1831–1837," *Civil War History* (December 1971). Much of the structure of this chapter and the one which follows it is outlined in this article. The long collaboration between English and American abolitionists is treated in Betty L. Fladeland, *Men and Brothers: Anglo-American Antislavery Cooperation* (1972). Biographies of the major white immediatists who emerged in the 1830's include John L. Thomas, *The Liberator, William Lloyd Garrison: A Biography* (1963); Bertram Wyatt-Brown, *Lewis Tappan and the Evangelical War against Slavery* (1969); Betty Fladeland, *James Gillespie Birney: Slaveholder to Abolitionist* (1955); Benjamin P. Thomas, *Theodore Weld, Crusader for Freedom* (1950); Ralph Volney Harlow, *Gerrit Smith, Philanthropist and Reformer* (1939); Merton Dillon, *Elijah P. Lovejoy, Abolitionist Editor* (1961); Robert Meredith, *The Politics of the Universe: Edward Beecher, Abolition and Orthodoxy* (1968); Jane H. and William H. Pease, *Bound with Them in Chains: A Biographical History of the Antislavery Movement* (1972); Richard Hofstadter, "Wendell Phillips, The Patrician as Agitator," in *The American Political Tradition and the Men Who Made It* (1948); Gerda Lerner, *The Grimké Sisters from South Carolina: Rebels against Slavery* (1967); Katherine Du Pré Lumpkin, *The Emancipation of Angelina Grimké* (1974); and Milton Meltzer, *Tongue of Flame: The Life of Lydia Maria Child* (1965).

The abolitionists' moral-suasion projects of the 1830's receive comprehensive treatment in many of the biographies just noted. Carleton Mabee's *Black Freedom: The Nonviolent Abolitionists from 1830 to the Civil War* (1970), is the most detailed study of the subject; Gilbert H. Barnes, *Antislavery Impulse* (1934), remains the most zestful, and Peter Brock, *Radical Pacifists in Antebellum America* (1968), contains pertinent chapters. On the postal campaign specifically, see Bertram Wyatt-Brown, "The Abolitionists' Postal Campaign of 1835," *Journal of Negro History* (October 1963). The South's hostile responses to moral suasion are detailed in Clement Eaton, *The Freedom of Thought Struggle in the Old South* (1940); Joseph C. Robert, *The Road From Monticello: The Virginia Slavery Debate of 1832* (1970); Eugene Genovese, *The World the*

Slaveholders Made (1970); and William Freehling, *Prelude to Civil War* (1966).

Northern antiabolitionism receives an essential contextual setting in racism and violence in the following studies: Leon Litwack, *North of Slavery* (1960); George Fredrickson, *Black Image* (1971); David Brion Davis, "Some Themes of Countersubversion: An Analysis of Anti-Catholic, Anti-Mormon and Anti-foreign Literature," *Mississippi Valley Historical Review* (September 1960), and "Some Ideological Functions of Prejudice in Antebellum America," *American Quarterly* (Summer 1963); and David Grimsted, "Rioting in Its Jacksonian Setting," *American Historical Review* (February 1973). Leonard Richards, *"Gentlemen of Property and Standing": Anti-Abolition Mobs in Jacksonian America* (1970), addresses the broad questions of the social status of the abolitionists and their mob opponents, the content of mob ideology, and the collective behavior of the mobs.

4. Petitions, Perfectionists, and Political Abolitionists

The growing involvement of abolitionism with issues of economics, politics, and civil liberties is described in Russel B. Nye, *Fettered Freedom: Civil Liberties and the Slavery Controversy, 1830–1860* (1949); Larry Gara, "Slavery and the Slave Power: A Crucial Distinction," *Civil War History* (March 1969); and Julian Bretz, "The Economic Background of the Liberty Party," *American Historical Review* (January 1929). A pivotal study, analyzing the process by which abolitionism mingled with the broad development of a Northern free-labor ideology in politics, is Eric Foner, *Free Soul, Free Labor, Free Men: The Ideology of the Republican Party before the Civil War* (1970). Gilbert H. Barnes, *Antislavery Impulse* (1934), stresses the "broadening impulse" of abolitionism in politics, while David Brion Davis, *The Slave Power Conspiracy and the Paranoid Style* (1969), analyzes the ever-spreading belief in political plotting among Southerners and Yankees.

For the impacts of violence on abolitionism, the gag-rule struggles, and the rise of political antislavery, the following are pertinent: James Brewer Stewart, "Peaceful Hopes and Violent Experiences: The Evolution of Radical and Reforming Abolitionism, 1831–1837," *Civil War History* (December 1971); John Demos, "The Anti-Slavery Movement and the Problem of Violent Means," *New England Quarterly* (December 1964); Sylvan Tompkins, "The Psychology of Commitment: The Constructive

Role of Violence and Suffering for the Individual and for His Society," in Martin Duberman (ed.), *The Antislavery Vanguard* (1965). The gag-rule struggles themselves are clearly described in Samuel Flagg Bemis, *John Quincy Adams and the Union* (1956); and James M. McPherson, "The Fight against the Gag Rule: Joshua Leavitt and the Antislavery Insurgency in the Whig Party, 1839–1842," *Journal of Negro History* (July 1963).

The social and regional boundaries of antislavery constituencies are suggested strongly in Leonard Richards, *"Gentlemen of Property and Standing"* (1970); Eric Foner, *Free Soil, Free Labor, Free Men* (1970); and Whitney Cross, *The Burnt-Over District* (1950). Other works which offer suggestive material include several articles by John L. Myers, "The Early Antislavery Agency System in Pennsylvania, 1833–1837," *Pennsylvania History* (March 1964); "The Major Effect of Antislavery Agencies in Vermont, 1832–1836," *Vermont History* (September 1968); "The Beginnings of Antislavery Agencies in New Hampshire, 1832–1835," *Historical New Hampshire* (March 1970); Robert Ludlum, *Social Ferment in Vermont* (1939); Harlan Hatcher, *The Western Reserve* (1960), and a number of biographies of antislavery figures in the politics of the 1840's, cited below under Chapter 5.

A study of the collision between conservative and radical abolitionists during the late 1830's, along with an extended, persuasive analysis of the two factions' conflicting assumptions, goals, and tactics, is found in Aileen Kraditor, *Means and Ends in American Abolitionism: Garrison and His Critics on Strategy and Tactics, 1834–1850* (1969).

5. Abolitionists and the Rise of the Free-Soil Movement

Insufficient attention has been given to studying abolitionist political tactics and their effectiveness. Most useful is Aileen Kraditor, *Means and Ends in American Abolitionism* (1969). James Brewer Stewart, *Joshua Giddings and the Tactics of Radical Politics* (1970), and "The Aims and Impact of Garrisonian Abolitionism, 1840–1860," *Civil War History* (September 1969); and Howard Zinn, "Abolitionists, Freedom Riders and the Tactics of Agitation," in Martin Duberman (ed.), *The Antislavery Vanguard* (1965), also assess strategies and tactics. Richard H. Sewell, *Ballots for Freedom* (1976), replaces Theodore C. Smith, *The Liberty and Free Soil Parties in the Northwest* (1897), as the clearest detailed inquiry into political abolitionism in the 1840's and 1850's.

The interplay of revivalism, radical abolitionism, and American Protestantism during the 1840's and 1850's is studied in Donald G. Matthews, *Slavery and Methodism: A Chapter in American Morality* (1965), and Timothy L. Smith, *Revivalism and Social Reform in Mid-Nineteenth-Century America* (1957). Especially stimulating is Lewis Perry, *Radical Abolitionism: Anarchy and the Government of God in Antislavery Thought* (1973).

The literature on westward expansion, the war with Mexico, and the accompanying sectional tensions is very large. Fredrick Merk, *Manifest Destiny* (1956), and Don Fehrenbacher, *The Era of Expansion, 1800–1848* (1969), provide useful starting points. Rising Northern sectionalism in politics is analyzed in terms of racism in the following works: Eugene Berwanger, *The Frontier against Slavery: Anti-Negro Prejudice and the Slavery Extension Controversy* (1967); Martin Duberman, "The Northern Response to Slavery," in Martin Duberman (ed.), *The Antislavery Vanguard* (1965); Eric Foner, "Politics and Prejudice: The Free Soil Party and the Negro, 1849–1852," *Journal of Negro History* (October 1965). Broader analysis of Northern ideology is found in two works of unusual importance: Major L. Wilson, *Time, Space and Freedom: The Quest for Nationality and the Irrepressible Conflict 1815–1861* (1974), and Eric Foner, *Free Soil, Free Labor, Free Men* (1970). The political narrative of free-soilism gets extended treatment in Joseph G. Rayback, *Free Soil: The Election of 1848* (1970); Fredrick J. Blue, *The Free Soilers: Third-Party Politics, 1848–1854* (1973); Chaplin W. Morrison, *Democratic Politics and Sectionalism: The Wilmot Proviso Controversy* (1968); and Eric Foner "The Wilmot Proviso Revisited," *Journal of American History* (September 1969). Southern motivations for slave expansion are best explained in Eugene Genovese, *The Political Economy of Slavery* (1967).

There are many biographies of the sectional politicians who began rising to prominence in the North during the 1840's; among the most useful are: Martin Duberman, *Charles Francis Adams* (1960); Frank O. Gatell, *John Gorham Palfrey and the New England Conscience* (1963); David Donald, *Charles Sumner and the Coming of the Civil War* (1960); Richard H. Sewell, *John P. Hale and the Politics of Abolition* (1965); Richard H. Abbott, *Cobbler in Congress: The Life of Henry Wilson* (1971); Charles B. Going, *David Wilmot, Free Soiler* (1934); Glyndon Van Deusen, *William Henry Seward* (1967); and John A. Garrity, *Silas Wright* (1948). Charles G. Sellers, *James K. Polk, Continentalist, 1843–1846* (1966), and Richard Current, *Daniel Webster and the Rise of National Conservatism* (1968), offer additional perspectives on the free-soil controversy. Holman Hamilton, *Prologue to Conflict: The Crisis and Compromise of 1850* (1964), is a clear, short analysis.

6. Race, Class, and Freedom in American Abolitionism

The complex history of the black abolitionists, their activities, ideas, and relationships with whites is best entered through Jane H. and William H. Pease's excellent *They Who Would Be Free: Blacks' Search For Freedom, 1831–1861* (1974). Another worthwhile introduction is Benjamin Quarles, *The Black Abolitionists* (1969). Benjamin Quarles, *Frederick Douglass* (1948); Edward Farrison, *William Wells Brown: Author and Reformer* (1969); and Cyril Griffith, *African Dream: Martin Delany and the Emergence of Pan-African Thought* (1975), are the major biographies of black abolitionists. Shorter biographical treatments of note include Jane H. and William H. Pease, "The Black Militant: Henry Highland Garnet" and "The Negro Conservative: Samuel Eli Cornish," in *Bound with Them in Chains* (1972); Donald Jacobs, "David Walker, Boston Race Leader," *Essex Institute Historical Bulletin* (January 1971); and Robert P. Smith, "William C. Nell, Crusading Black Abolitionist," *Journal of Negro History* (July 1970). A considerable number of autobiographical slave narratives have also been reprinted. Among the most useful are those by Frederick Douglass, Austin Steward, William Wells Brown, Josiah Henson, Henry Bibb, James W. C. Pennington, and Samuel Ringgold Ward.

Race relations between black and white abolitionists are examined in the following: Leon Litwack "The Emancipation of the Negro Abolitionist," in Martin Duberman (ed.), *The Antislavery Vanguard* (1965); Jane H. and William H. Pease "Ends, Means and Attitudes: Black-White Conflict in the Antislavery Movement," *Civil War History* (June 1972). Expressions of black nationalism are examined in Floyd J. Miller, *The Search for a Black Nationality: Black Emigration and Colonization, 1787–1863* (1975).

Black cooperation with whites in opposing discrimination is stressed in Carleton Mabee, *Black Freedom* (1970), while Larry Gara's *Liberty Line: The Legend of the Underground Railroad* (1961), documents the blacks' self-sufficiency in aiding fugitive slaves. Howard Bell, *A Survey of the Negro Convention Movement, 1830–1861* (1969), explores black self-help programs of a different sort. David M. Katzman, *Before the Ghetto: Black Detroit in the Nineteenth Century* (1973), offers a clear picture of the oppressive circumstances against which Northern urban blacks had to contend. Leon Litwack, *North of Slavery: The Negro in the Free States, 1790–1860* (1960), offers a more general description of white supremacist practices.

7. Abolitionists and the Coming of the Civil War

On the interplay of Northern party loyalty with sectional ideology during the early 1850's, different perspectives are offered by Joel Silby, *The Shrine of Party: Congressional Voting Behavior, 1841–1852* (1967), and Fredrick Blue, *The Free Soilers* (1973). Regarding the abolitionists' increasing willingness to employ violent means, see Lewis Perry, *Radical Abolitionism* (1973); Chapter X of Merton Dillon, *The Abolitionists: The Growth of a Dissenting Minority* (1973); and Jane H. and William H. Pease, "Confrontation and Abolition in the 1850's," *Journal of American History* (March 1972). The 1850 Fugitive Slave Law, its enforcement, and its political implications are discussed in Stanley Campbell, *The Slave-catchers: The Enforcement of the Fugitive Slave Law* (1968), and Jane H. and William H. Pease, *The Fugitive Slave Law and Anthony Burns: A Problem in Law Enforcement* (1975).

A number of biographies are particularly pertinent to the political fragmentation and violence of the 1850's: Henry S. Commager, *Theodore Parker: Yankee Crusader* (1947); Tilden Edelstein, *Strange Enthusiasm: A Life of Thomas Wentworth Higginson* (1968); Harold Schwartz, *Samuel Gridley Howe* (1959); Steven Oates, *To Purge This Land with Blood: A Biography of John Brown* (1970); Richard O. Boyer, *The Legend of John Brown* (1974); Fawn Brodie, *Thaddeus Stevens, Scourge of the South* (1959); Patrick Riddleburger, *George Washington Julian, Radical Republican* (1966); Edward Magdol, *Owen Lovejoy: Abolitionist in Congress* (1967); Hans Trefousse, *Benjamin Franklin Wade: Radical Republican from Ohio* (1963); Robert W. Johannson, *Stephen A. Douglas* (1973); and Benjamin P. Thomas, *Abraham Lincoln* (1952). A number of the biographies listed above for Chapter 5 are also valuable for the 1850's. Harriet Beecher Stowe and *Uncle Tom's Cabin* receive perceptive treatment in Edmund Wilson, *Patriotic Gore: Studies in the Literature of the American Civil War* (1966).

For the complex history of the Kansas issue and its impact on politics, see James Rawley, *Race and Politics: "Bleeding Kansas" and the Coming of the Civil War* (1969), while Ronald Takaki, *A Pro-Slavery Crusade: The*

Agitation to Re-open the African Slave Trade (1970), analyzes some of the motives for aggressive Southern expansionism in the 1850's. Racist aspects of free-soil ideology and the pre-war Republican Party are treated in Eugene Berwanger, *The Frontier against Slavery* (1967). Michael Holt, *Forging a Majority: The Formation of the Republican Party in Pittsburgh, 1848–1860* (1969), and Ronald P. Formisano, *The Birth of Mass Political Parties: Michigan, 1827–1861* (1971), present different views of nativism and Republican politics from those developed in this book. Eric Foner, *Free Soil, Free Labor, Free Men* (1970), is an extended analysis of the Republican coalition's several components and of the ideology which brought them together.

Two recent articles make some much-needed sense of Abraham Lincoln's views on slavery and race equality: George Fredrickson, "A Man but Not a Brother: Abraham Lincoln and Race Equality," *Journal of Southern History* (February 1975); and Don E. Fehrenbacher, "Only His Stepchildren: Lincoln and the Negro," in George Fredrickson (ed.), *A Nation Divided* (1975). A useful historiographical treatment of the causes of the Civil War is Thomas J. Pressley, *Americans Interpret Their Civil War* (1954).

8. Triumph and Tragedy. Abolitionists and Emancipation

A useful historiographical essay which views abolitionism from the standpoint of Reconstruction is Richard O. Curry, "The Abolitionists and Reconstruction: A Critical Appraisal," *Journal of Southern History* (November 1968). James M. McPherson, *The Struggle for Equality: The Abolitionists and the Negro in the Civil War and Reconstruction* (1964), details immediatist activity from 1861 through the end of that decade. V. Jacques Voegli, *Free but Not Equal: The Negro in the Midwest during the Civil War and Reconstruction* (1967), and Forrest Wood, *Black Scare: The Racist Response to Emancipation and Reconstruction* (1970), both emphasize the continuity of white supremacism in Northern politics after 1861.

Black political activism, military participation, and other experiences during the Civil War and afterward can be followed in James M. McPherson (ed.), *The Negro's Civil War* (1965); Dudley Cornish, *The Sable Arm* (1956); Peter Kolchin, *First Freedom: The Response of Alabama's Blacks to Emancipation and Reconstruction* (1972); and Otis Singletary, *The Negro Militia and Reconstruction* (1957). The history of the Freedmen's Bureau is presented from conflicting viewpoints in William McFeeley, *Yankee Stepfather: General O. O. Howard and the Freedmen* (1968); Martin Abbott, *The Freedmen's Bureau in South Carolina* (1967); and La Wanda Cox, "General O. O. Howard and the 'Misrepresented Bureau,' " *Journal of Southern History* (November 1953).

John Hope Franklin, ed., *The Emancipation Proclamation* (1963), traces the Republican evolution from traditional unionism to emancipation. Robert Cruden, *The Negro in Reconstruction* (1969), is a convenient survey. Willie Lee Rose, *Rehearsal for Reconstruction: The Port Royal Experiment* (1964), and Joel Williamson, *After Slavery* (1965), furnish many insights on the transition "from slavery to freedom". Rose's book also suggests the nature of the war's impact upon abolitionists. This latter topic is of central concern in George Fredrickson, *The Inner Civil War: Northern Intellectuals and the Crisis of the Union* (1965).

For the politics of Reconstruction, the role of Andrew Johnson, and the limits of Republican radicalism, see Eric McKittrick, *Andrew Johnson and Reconstruction* (1960); Michael Les Benedict, *A Compromise of Principle* (1974); W. R. Brock, *An American Crisis: Congress and Reconstruction 1865–1867* (1963); and C. Vann Woodward, "Seeds of Failure: The Radical Race Policy," in Harold Hyman (ed.) *New Frontiers in Reconstruction* (1966). On the waning of Reconstruction, good general treatments are Vincent P. De Santis, *Republicans Face the Southern Question* (1959), and Stanley Hirshson, *Farewell to the Bloody Shirt* (1962). The linkages between abolitionism and later civil rights movements is explored in James M. McPherson, *The Abolitionist Legacy: From Reconstruction to the NAACP* (1976).

Finally, abolitionists are shown contemplating the ambiguous outcome of their crusade in Larry Gara, "A Glorious Time: The 1874 Abolitionist Reunion in Chicago," *Journal of the Illinois State Historical Society* (Autumn 1972). Merton Dillon examines the same topic in "The Failure of the American Abolitionists," *Journal of Southern History* (March 1959).

Index

[217]